COMPREHENSION AND GRAMMAR

YEAR 6

PASCAL PRESS

CONTENTS

Term 1

Fiction Unit

Lexile Levels 980L–1010L

Nonfiction Unit

Lexile Levels 990L–1020L

Term 2

Fiction Unit

Lexile Levels 1010L–1050L

Nonfiction Unit

Lexile Levels 1020L–1080L

Term 3

Fiction Unit

Lexile Levels 1050L–1100L

Nonfiction Unit

Lexile Levels 1080L–1150L

Term 4

Fiction Unit

Lexile Levels 1100L–1150L

Nonfiction Unit

Lexile Levels 1150L–1200L

INTRODUCTION

Reading comprehension is the ability to understand and interpret text. To become confident and competent readers, students need to learn how to understand the literal meaning of a text and its vocabulary, and also its implied and inferred meaning.

This workbook is organised into four terms of work with 40 step-by-step lessons that focus on specific comprehension skills. To further support students, 8 grammar lessons target language usage. By looking carefully at words, clauses and sentences, students are better equipped to understand the texts they read. Each terms ends with a summative assessment that identifies students' strengths and rewards progress.

Step-by-step Comprehension

The 40 comprehension lessons teach key strategies for students to use when they read. Each lesson uses a levelled extract and focuses on a single comprehension strategy, with clear, easy-to-read instructions.

Students find key details in the text and highlight words and phrases. This ensures students have knowledge of the text before answering comprehension questions. The extracts are organised in a progressive sequence with clear modelling and built-in support. By focusing on a single strategy at a time, students develop their literal, inferential and critical comprehension skills, as well as extending their vocabulary.

Integrated Grammar

The eight grammar lessons in this book aim to help students understand how the English language system works, and how to apply this knowledge to texts.

Each lesson teaches a key concept in grammar. The focus is on connecting grammatical terms to text in meaningful ways. The instructional information box explains the concept and shows examples. Students then annotate a text and answer questions to identify the grammar in action. Questions increase in difficulty and include NAPLAN-style questions. The grammar lessons help students comprehend and connect with a broad range of texts.

The Reading Eggspress Online Lessons

Reading Eggspress provides a comprehensive and systematic online program that models, scaffolds and supports reading comprehension. The 220 lessons have been organised in a clear progression to develop reading comprehension skills for students in Years 1–6. Each lesson includes built-in motivational elements to reward efforts and boost students' enthusiasm for reading.

The workbook lessons can be completed as a stand-alone reading comprehension course, but when combined with the online lessons they act as a powerful boost to students' reading comprehension skills. Students using the online program show significant year-on-year improvements in both reading comprehension skills and higher reading levels, as highlighted in the program's detailed reporting module.

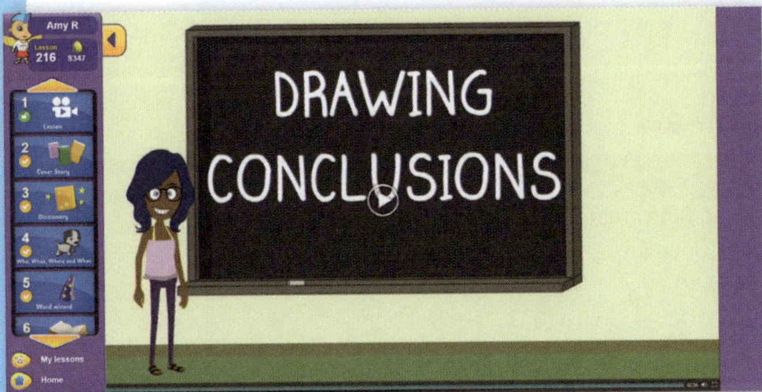

Engaging lessons

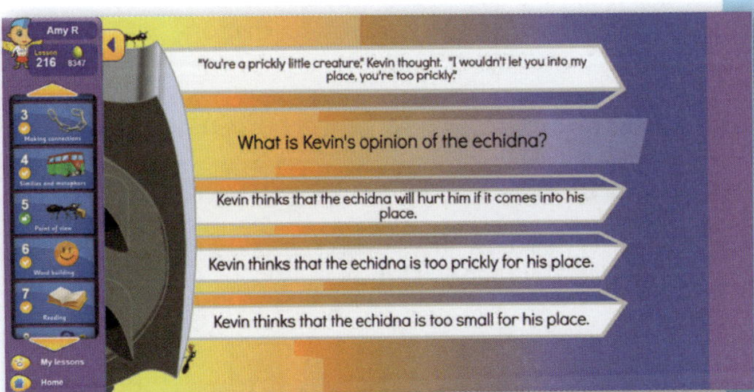

Interactive activities

The Library 4000+ ebooks

Students can practise their comprehension skills by reading ebooks in the Reading Eggspress Library. Search by topic, series, author, Lexile, reading age or book title to find the perfect book. With illustrated chapter books, full colour nonfiction books, poetry collections and a range of classics, there are texts to suit all readers and their capabilities.

New titles are added regularly with audio for all lower level books.

The Stadium

Compete in real time against students from around the country and around the world. These exciting head-to-head contests test skills in one of four areas—spelling, vocabulary, usage or grammar.

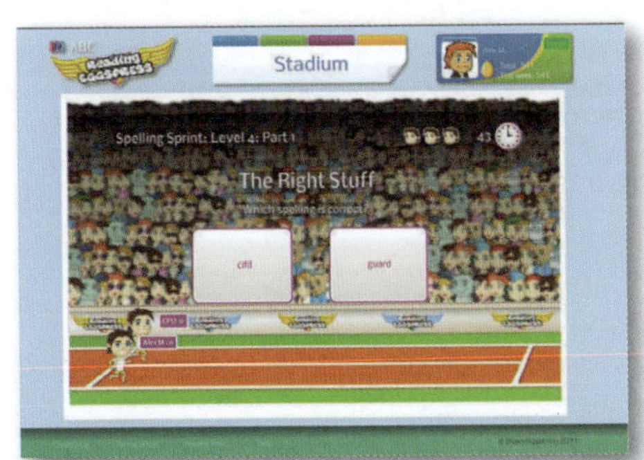

Reading Eggspress Workbooks and the Australian Curriculum

Each workbook lesson focuses on a core comprehension strategy or key concept in grammar. The texts, strategies and concepts were developed to align with the Australian Curriculum.

Year 6 Literacy

Analysing, interpreting and evaluating

AC9E6LY03 Analyse how text structures and language features work together to meet the purpose of a text, and engage and influence audiences

AC9E6LY04 Select, navigate and read texts for a range of purposes, monitoring meaning and evaluating the use of structural features; for example, table of contents, glossary, chapters, headings and subheadings

AC9E6LY05 Use comprehension strategies such as visualising, predicting, connecting, summarising, monitoring and questioning to build literal and inferred meaning, and to connect and compare content from a variety of sources

Year 6 Language

Text structure and organisation

AC9E6LA03 Explain how texts across the curriculum are typically organised into characteristic stages and phases depending on purposes, recognising how authors often adapt text structures and language features

Language for expressing and developing ideas

AC9E6LA05 Understand how embedded clauses can expand the variety of complex sentences to elaborate, extend and explain ideas

AC9E6LA06 Understand how ideas can be expanded and sharpened through careful choice of verbs, elaborated tenses and a range of adverb groups

AC9E6LA07 Identify and explain how images, figures, tables, diagrams, maps and graphs contribute to meaning

AC9E6LA08 Identify authors' use of vivid, emotive vocabulary, such as metaphors, similes, personification, idioms, imagery and hyperbole

Reading Eggspress Comprehension Strategy Overview

Comprehension	Strategy	Fiction Lessons	Nonfiction Lessons
Literal Looks for explicitly stated answers in the texts. Answers **Who**, **What**, **When** and **Where** questions.	Finding Facts and Information	192, 203	
	Main Idea and Details		187, 198
	Sequencing Events		208, 217
	Reading Diagrams		200, 220
Inferential Finds implied information in the text. Looks for **text clues** and evidence that point to the correct answer.	Cause and Effect	204, 211	197, 210
	Compare and Contrast		196, 216
	Drawing Conclusions	182, 215	218
	Making Inferences	183	206
	Making Predictions	201	
	Figurative Language	194, 214	
	Summarising	185, 191, 202	
Critical Asks for **connections** or **opinions** on information in the text. Uses text clues to support the connections.	Analysing Character Actions	181	
	Making Connections	213	189, 219
	Visualisation	205	
	Point of View	212	188,
	Audience and Purpose	184, 193	199
	Fact or Opinion?		190, 209
Vocabulary Uses context clues and own knowledge to understand key words in the text.	Word Study	195	186, 207

Reading Eggspress Grammar Overview

Grammar	Focus	Fiction Lessons	Nonfiction Lessons
Sentence Looks at how **clauses** are structured and how they come together to **build** cohesive sentences.	Adjective Phrases	1	
	Active and Passive Voice		4
	Multi-clause Sentences	5	
	Adjectival Clauses		6
	Verb Phrases	7	
Text Assesses paragraph **composition** to see how sentences work together to create cohesive texts.	Perfect Continuous Tense	3	
	Future Tense		8
Punctuation Models correct punctuation **usage** for different types of words, clauses and sentences.	Dashes and Semi-colons		2

STUDENT RECORD SHEET

Use this page to record the number of questions you answered correctly for each lesson.

Term 1

Map 37 Fiction Lessons 980L–1010L	**181** Analysing Character Actions	**182** Drawing Conclusions	**183** Making Inferences	**184** Audience and Purpose	**185** Summarising	**Grammar 1** Adjective Phrases	
Map 38 Nonfiction Lessons 990L–1020L	**186** Word Study	**187** Main Idea and Details	**188** Point of View	**189** Making Connections	**190** Fact or Opinion?	**Grammar 2** Dashes and Semi-colons	**Assessment 1** *Computer Annihilation*

Term 2

Map 39 Fiction Lessons 1010L–1050L	**191** Summarising	**192** Finding Facts and Information	**193** Audience and Purpose	**194** Figurative Language	**195** Word Study	**Grammar 3** Perfect Continuous Tense	
Map 40 Nonfiction Lessons 1020L–1080L	**196** Compare and Contrast	**197** Cause and Effect	**198** Main Idea and Details	**199** Audience and Purpose	**200** Reading Diagrams	**Grammar 4** Active and Passive Voice	**Assessment 2** *Antarctic Explorers*

Term 3

Map 41 Fiction Lessons 1050L–1100L	**201** Making Predictions	**202** Summarising	**203** Finding Facts and Information	**204** Cause and Effect	**205** Visualisation	**Grammar 5** Multi-clause Sentences	
Map 42 Nonfiction Lessons 1080L–1150L	**206** Making Inferences	**207** Word Study	**208** Sequencing Events	**209** Fact or Opinion?	**210** Cause and Effect	**Grammar 6** Adjectival Clauses	**Assessment 3** *The Snake-haired Monster*

Term 4

Map 43 Fiction Lessons 1100L–1150L	**211** Cause and Effect	**212** Point of View	**213** Making Connections	**214** Figurative Language	**215** Drawing Conclusions	**Grammar 7** Verb Phrases	
Map 44 Nonfiction Lessons 1150L–1200L	**216** Compare and Contrast	**217** Sequencing Events	**218** Drawing Conclusions	**219** Making Connections	**220** Reading Diagrams	**Grammar 8** The Future Tense	**Assessment 4** *Gorillas*

LESSON 181

On the Trail of the Golden Man

Interpreting Character Behaviour, Feelings and Motivation

To interpret a character's feelings and what motivates them to behave in a certain way, you need to look for clues in the text. The clues are usually in the words and punctuation.

Read the passage.

Put a box around how Mia and Flynn felt with Sipu around.

Underline a sentence that demonstrates Sipu's survival skills.

Sipu made walking through the jungle look easy. It wasn't scary with Sipu around. This was his home. He had grown up here. Sipu thought nothing of climbing over tree roots double his height, breaking vines for a quick drink and climbing up a tree for a bite to eat. He walked so lightly through the forest his feet barely marked the ground. He showed Mia and Flynn how to walk through the rainforest without being seen or heard.

Colour how Sipu moved through the jungle.

Highlight what Mia and Flynn learnt from Sipu.

Circle the correct answers.

1. Based on evidence in the passage, which sentence best describes Sipu? Sipu …
   - a has excellent survival skills.
   - b has good time management skills.
   - c is very competitive.
   - d has extraordinary strength.
2. What is the **clue** to question 1's answer? Sipu is able to …
   - a walk lightly through the jungle.
   - b stay warm in the jungle.
   - c find food and water in the jungle.
   - d identify plants and animals in the jungle.
3. Which sentence best sums up Sipu's **attitude** towards Mia and Flynn? Sipu …
   - a thinks he's smarter than Mia and Flynn.
   - b wants to share his knowledge.
   - c wants to learn from Mia and Flynn.
   - d thinks Mia and Flynn are a nuisance.
4. Which word is the best **clue** to question 3's answer?
   - a easy
   - b showed
   - c nothing
   - d scary
5. How did Mia and Flynn **feel** with Sipu as their guide?
   - a scared
   - b disappointed
   - c relaxed
   - d confused

AC9E6LY05 Use comprehension strategies such as connecting to build inferred meaning

Read the passage.

Circle the word Flynn uses to describe the moon.

Highlight Sipu's gift to Mia and Flynn.

"Hey, look guys!" cried Flynn, pointing to the sky. It was dark now and the moon sat full in the night sky. It looked strangely golden. "Doesn't that look awesome?"

The strange coloured moonlight was making them all look golden. El Dorado was with them. Flynn and Mia thought about Sipu and his secret tribe and the great gift that he had given them. He had shown them some of the real treasures of the rainforest, and they would keep their word and do whatever they could to protect it. Their visit to El Dorado would remain a treasured secret forever.

Underline how Flynn and Mia intend to repay Sipu.

Colour the words that help us to understand how Flynn and Mia feel about El Dorado.

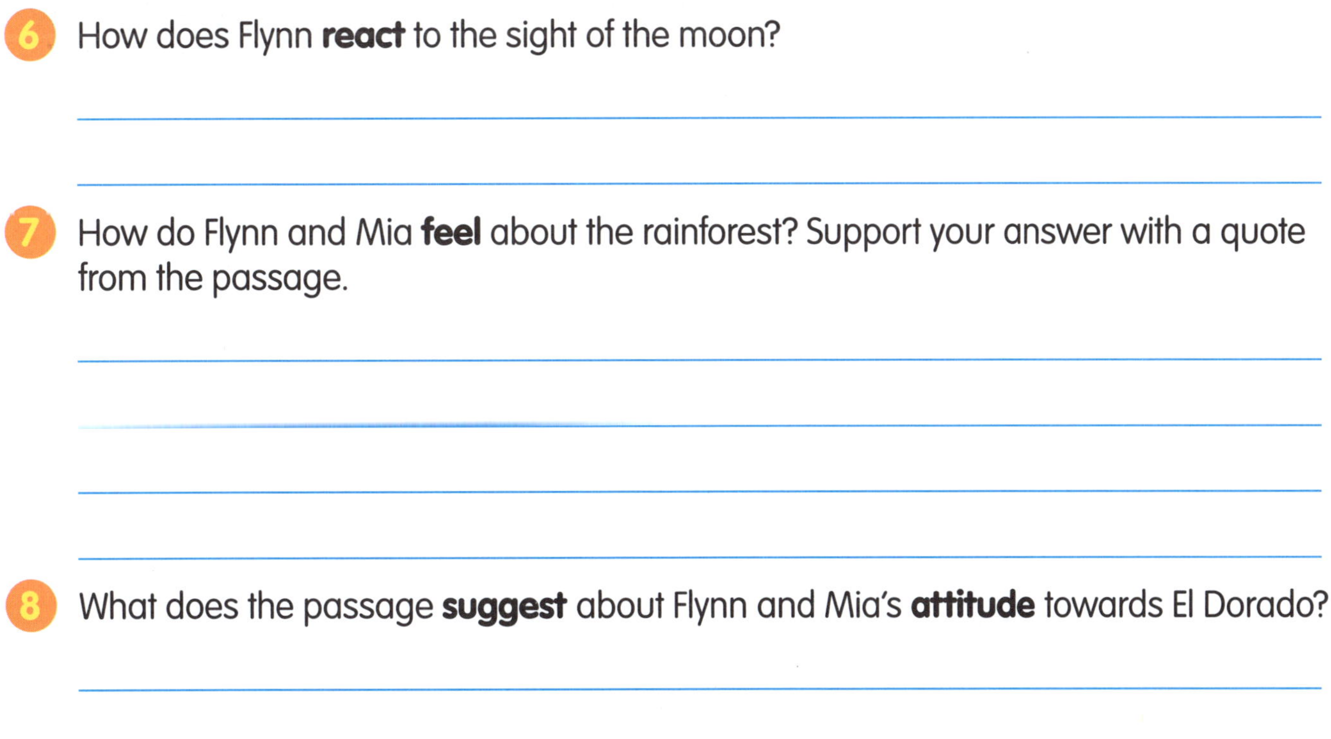

6 How does Flynn **react** to the sight of the moon?

7 How do Flynn and Mia **feel** about the rainforest? Support your answer with a quote from the passage.

8 What does the passage **suggest** about Flynn and Mia's **attitude** towards El Dorado?

LESSON 182

In the Clear?

Drawing Conclusions

To draw conclusions from a text, we have to use clues to make our own judgements. The clues help us find the answers that are hiding in the text.

Read the passage.

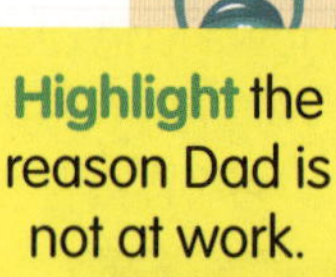

Highlight the reason Dad is not at work.

Underline the event the residents of Sunset Heights will be celebrating.

Colour the question Mum asks Nick.

Put a box around Nick's reply.

In the final sentence, circle the word that can be replaced with *said*.

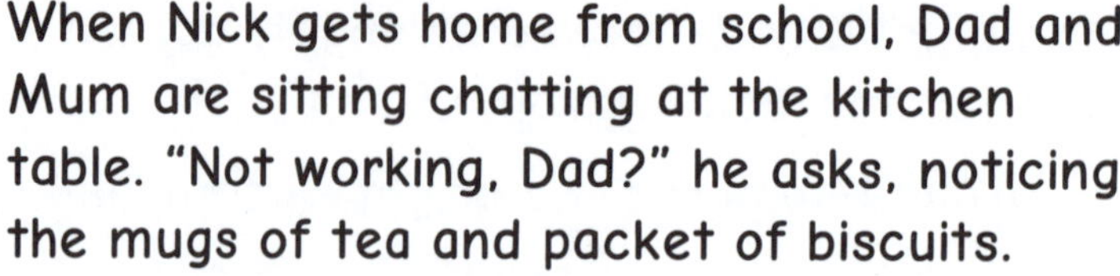

When Nick gets home from school, Dad and Mum are sitting chatting at the kitchen table. "Not working, Dad?" he asks, noticing the mugs of tea and packet of biscuits.

"I knocked off early to give Mum a hand moving furniture at Sunset Heights. It's Mrs Blessop's ninetieth birthday party tomorrow," Dad explains.

"Will you lend a hand too, Nick? There are a dozen trestle tables to be shifted," Mum asks when he sits down at the table.

Nick sighs, "Yeah, I'll help."

Circle the correct answers.

1. Which is the best **conclusion**? Sunset Heights is …
   - a a hotel.
   - b a retirement home.
   - c an apartment block.
   - d a hospital.
2. Which phrase is the **clue** to question 1's answer?
   - a knocked off early
   - b a dozen trestle tables
   - c at the table
   - d ninetieth birthday party
3. Which is the best **conclusion**? Nick …
   - a is excited about helping Mum.
   - b is unenthusiastic about helping Mum.
   - c refuses to help Mum.
   - d does not think he can help Mum.
4. Which word is the best **clue** to question 3's answer?
   - a sighs
   - b Yeah
   - c help
   - d I'll
5. What can we **conclude** about Mum's connection to Sunset Heights?
   - a Mum's parents live there.
   - b Mrs Blessop is Mum's best friend.
   - c Mum helps out there.
   - d Mum has known Mrs Blessop all her life.

AC9E6LY05 Use comprehension strategies such as connecting to build inferred meaning

Read the passage.

Highlight the sentence that suggests Nick meant to take the long way.

Underline the description of the Flemings' garden.

Circle the words that describe the SUV.

Colour Nick's description of his house.

Nick walks to Sunset Heights the long way. His feet are in charge and just happen to be taking him this way.

When he gets to Laura Fleming's house, Nick scans the large garden with its manicured lawns, tall trees and rose beds. There's a Saab parked on the gravel drive and also a new, red SUV. Nick notices a couple of builders mixing concrete near the front steps.

Nick thinks of his dad, who works hard every day, but doesn't seem to get very much—just a boring little house and not much else.

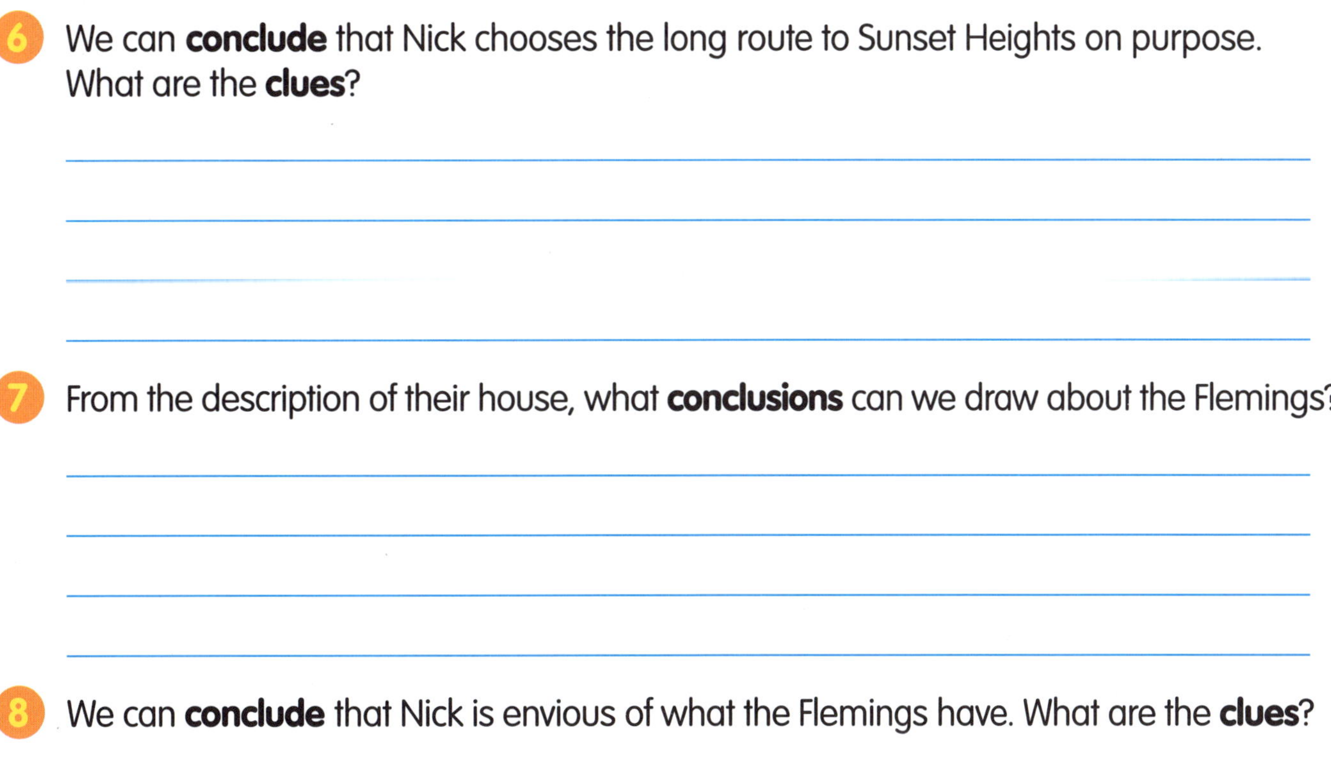

6 We can **conclude** that Nick chooses the long route to Sunset Heights on purpose. What are the **clues**?

7 From the description of their house, what **conclusions** can we draw about the Flemings?

8 We can **conclude** that Nick is envious of what the Flemings have. What are the **clues**?

LESSON 183

Digging for Buried Treasure

Making Inferences

To make inferences while reading, we have to use clues in the text. The clues help us find the answers that are hiding in the text.

Read the passage.

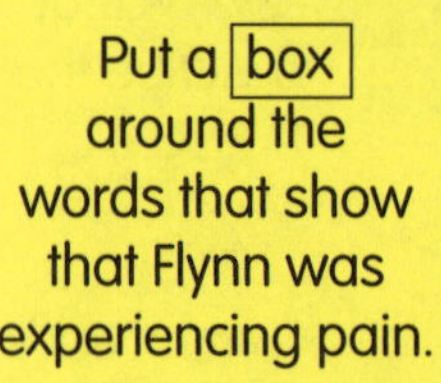

Put a box around the words that show that Flynn was experiencing pain.

Colour the words that suggest that Flynn and Mia had landed right next to each other.

They were spinning out of the marketplace and out of control.

"Ouch! Ouch! Ouch!" yelped Flynn, peeling Curiosity off his head. "Watch your claws, you dumb cat. Let go! Mia, move your elbow — it's breaking my ribs." Mia struggled to her feet. They had landed in bushes, on a dune behind a beach.

Hearing voices, they fell silent. They crawled to the top of the dune and peered over.

Underline where Flynn and Mia landed.

Highlight the sentence that helps us work out where the voices were coming from.

Circle the correct answers.

1. What do the words "Ouch! Ouch! Ouch!" **suggest**? Flynn …
   - a had landed safely.
   - b was spinning uncontrollably.
   - c had broken his ribs.
   - d was experiencing pain.
2. Which is the best **inference**? Flynn and Mia landed …
   - a far apart.
   - b opposite each other.
   - c close together.
   - d upside down.
3. Which group of words is the **clue** to question 2's answer?
   - a off his head
   - b landed in bushes
   - c out of control
   - d move your elbow
4. Which is the best **inference**? The voices were coming from …
   - a the beach.
   - b the top of the dune.
   - c the marketplace.
   - d the bushes.
5. What is the **clue** to question 4's answer? To see where the voices were coming from, Mia and Flynn had to …
   - a search in the bushes.
   - b crawl around the dune.
   - c peer over the dune.
   - d go back to the marketplace.

AC9E6LY05 Use comprehension strategies such as connecting to build inferred meaning

Read the passage.

Highlight the words that indicate the location of Oak Island.

Circle the name of the person who uncovered the site in 1795.

Colour the items that have been uncovered so far.

Oak Island is a small island off the coast of Nova Scotia, Canada. Legend says that treasure is buried in a pit on the island. In 1795, a teenager called Daniel McGinnis uncovered what he believed to be a site for buried treasure. With the help of friends he began to dig. They were forced to abandon their search, however, because the hole kept filling with water.

Over the next 200 years many different groups tried to find what was hidden in the pit. All the things uncovered so far are thought to be clues to bigger treasure — coins, gold chains, parchment and a stone with strange writing.

Underline the reason McGinnis and his friends were forced to abandon their search.

Colour the sentence that shows that people have continued to search for treasure on Oak Island.

6 What can we **infer** about the existence of buried treasure on Oak Island? Support your answer with quotes from the passage.

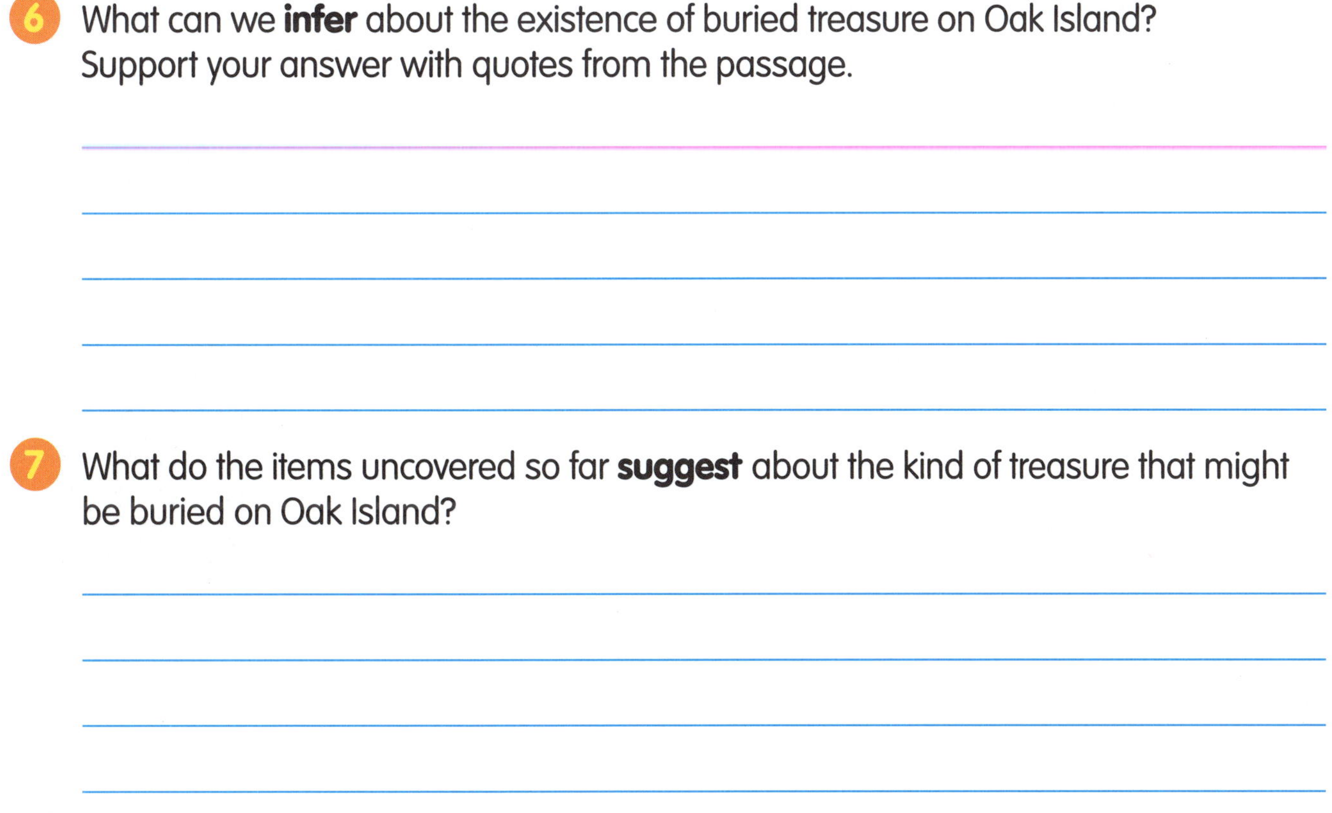

7 What do the items uncovered so far **suggest** about the kind of treasure that might be buried on Oak Island?

LESSON 184

Station Kuku

Identifying Audience and Purpose

To identify the author's purpose in writing a text, it helps to work out who the text was written for. The language the author uses will show what his or her purpose is—to inform, persuade, instruct, or entertain.

Read the passage.

Circle an example of an informal expression.

Underline an example of a rhetorical question.

Now folksies, tonight we are giving you a new feature—an extra service. Ladies and gentlemen of our vast unconscious audience, you have heard of jokes funny enough to make a horse laugh—well, that's the kind of jokes we want on this program, jokes funny enough to make a horse laugh, and in carrying out our policy of service to the people, beginning tonight we are bringing a horse into the studio to try our jokes out on. What other radio station would go to such lengths for its public?

Colour the words that help us work out what the purpose of the text is.

Highlight what the new feature on the program will be.

Circle the correct answers.

1. Who is the person making the announcement **addressing**? He is addressing people …
   - a watching television.
   - b in a theatre audience.
   - c listening to the radio.
   - d at a music festival.
2. What is the main **purpose** of the announcement? The purpose of the announcement is to …
   - a persuade people to listen to the program.
   - b inform people about a new feature on the program.
   - c warn people that there will be a horse on the program.
   - d entertain people with a joke about a horse.
3. Which word best describes the kind of **language** the announcer uses?
   - a persuasive
   - b emotive
   - c formal
   - d informal
4. Which word the announcer uses is the best **clue** to question 3's answer?
   - a folksies
   - b funny
   - c jokes
   - d laugh

AC9E6LY03 Analyse how text structures and language features work together to meet the purpose of a text

Read the passage.

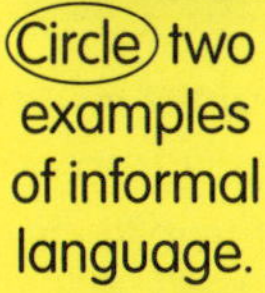

Highlight how the sound of a horse entering and running away is recreated.

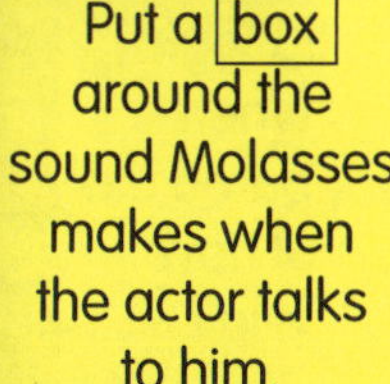

Underline an example of a script direction.

[Hoofs fade in. Note, use wooden hoofs.]

Come here, Molasses — whoa — whoa — all ready for work?

[Snort]

Good! Now, Molasses, I am going to tell you a joke.

[Snort and run away.]

Hey, bring that horse back here!

[Hoof in.]

Whoa! Molasses, you misunderstood me.

[Snort]

5 List two examples of informal language in the text.

6 How can we tell that this text is part of a play?

7 How can we tell that the play was written for a radio audience?

LESSON 185

How the Kangaroo Got Its Tail

Summarising

A summary is a shortened version of the original text. To summarise a text, you need to look for the points and details that contain the most important information.

Read the passage.

Highlight when Kangaroo did not have a tail.

Circle the relationship between Kangaroo and Wombat.

Colour where Kangaroo and Wombat slept at night.

Underline why Kangaroo asked Wombat to let him into his hut.

Long ago in the Dreamtime, Kangaroo did not have a tail. He was good friends with Wombat and they both lived in huts built from tree bark.

At night, Kangaroo liked to sleep outside where he could look up at the stars. He made fun of Wombat for always wanting to sleep inside the hut.

When winter came, Kangaroo still slept outside and teased Wombat about his smelly hut. But one night, rain fell so hard that each drop felt like a jab by a spear on Kangaroo's back. Kangaroo struggled against the wind to reach Wombat's hut.

"Let me in!" he cried.

Circle the correct answers.

1. Which sentence **summarises** the relationship between Kangaroo and Wombat?
   - a Long ago, Kangaroo did not have a tail.
   - b Long ago, Kangaroo and Wombat lived in huts.
   - c Long ago, Kangaroo and Wombat were good friends.
   - d Long ago, Kangaroo and Wombat built huts from wood bark.
2. Which sentence **summarises** the most important information in paragraph 2?
   - a Kangaroo liked to make fun of Wombat.
   - b Kangaroo liked to sleep outside, and Wombat liked to sleep in his hut.
   - c Kangaroo liked to look at the stars at night.
   - d Wombat liked to sleep in his hut at night.
3. Which sentence provides the **best summary** of the final paragraphs?
   - a Kangaroo continued to sleep outside even when the weather got colder.
   - b One night the rain fell so hard that it felt like a spear jabbing into Kangaroo's back.
   - c Kangaroo had to struggle against the wind to reach Wombat's hut.
   - d One winter's night it rained so hard that Kangaroo asked Wombat to let him into his hut.

AC9E6LY05 Use comprehension strategies such as summarising to build inferred meaning

Read the passage.

<u>Underline</u> why Kangaroo could not get dry or warm.

Highlight what Kangaroo did to Wombat in the morning.

Colour when Wombat threw the spear at Kangaroo.

Kangaroo lay in the corner. There was a hole in the wall, where wind and rain came in. He couldn't get dry or warm, and he grew angry as he watched Wombat enjoying a dream.

In the morning, Kangaroo was stiff and sore. He hobbled outside and picked up a large rock. He dropped the rock on Wombat's head, flattening his forehead and making his nose curl around.

Wombat planned his revenge. He waited until Kangaroo was busy washing and then he threw a spear at him. The spear landed at the base of Kangaroo's spine. Kangaroo tried to pull the spear out, but it was stuck.

"From now on, that will be your tail," yelled Wombat.

<u>Underline</u> where the spear landed.

Put a box around why Kangaroo could not remove the spear.

Circle what the spear turned into.

4 Complete the following summary by filling in important information from the passage.

a Kangaroo was cold and wet all night because ______________________________

____

______________________________.

b Kangaroo was cross with Wombat, so in the morning ______________________________

____

______________________________.

c Wombat got his revenge by ______________________________

____

______________________________.

d Kangaroo could not remove the spear, and ______________________________

______________________________.

GRAMMAR LESSON 1

Adjective Phrases

An **adjective phrase** is a group of words that does the work of an adjective. It gives information about a **noun**. For example: **The two white mice in the cage belong to my friend.** The adjective phrases **two white** and **in the cage** give information about the noun **mice**.

Read the extract.

Circle the **adjective** in the underlined phrase.

Underline the **adjective phrase** that gives information about the noun shop.

In the underlined phrase, put a box around the **noun** and colour the **adjective phrase**.

In the underlined phrase, circle the **noun** and highlight the **adjective phrase**.

Almost Twins

People said they were sorry about the fire, but that the Khans were very lucky to have escaped. They began discussing plans for a new, much bigger shop.

In the afternoon, Lela made her delicious coconut sponge with pink icing, and in the evening, the families gathered to sing "Happy Birthday" to Adi and Priya.

Finally, when all the village girls and women lined up on the lawn for their famous Fijian fan dance, Priya joined them. She was dressed in a brightly coloured sarong and grass skirt and held a beautifully woven fan. It was her birthday present from Adi.

"We are so fortunate to have such wonderful daughters, aren't we?" said Agnessi Kinitavaki, putting her arm around Lela Khan and squeezing hard.

Circle the correct answers.

In each sentence, identify the adjective phrase.

1. People said the Khans were very lucky to have escaped.
   - a People said
   - b the Khans
   - c very lucky
   - d have escaped
2. That afternoon, Lela made a delicious coconut sponge in Agnessi's kitchen.
   - a Lela made
   - b delicious coconut
   - c That afternoon
   - d Agnessi's kitchen
3. The girls and women lined up on the lawn for their famous Fijian dance.
   - a on the lawn
   - b girls and women
   - c lined up
   - d famous Fijian
4. Lela agreed that she and Agnessi were two very fortunate women.
   - a two very fortunate
   - b Lela agreed
   - c that she and
   - d Agnessi were
5. The fan Priya used in the dance was a present from Adi.
   - a The fan
   - b in the dance
   - c from Adi
   - d a present

AC9E6LA06 Understand how ideas can be expanded and sharpened

6 **Complete each sentence with an adjective phrase from the box below.**

a A cake ______________________________ will be hard to find.

b Priya's mother made a huge pot ______________________________.

c The dancers had to learn a number ______________________________ ______________________________.

d A girl holding a ______________________________ moved on to the dance floor.

e The fire had spread to the roof ______________________________.

f Their shop and house disappeared in a ball ______________________________ ______________________________.

of very strong tea	**of crimson flames**	**more delicious than this**
of the shop	**of very difficult steps**	**beautifully woven fan**

7 **Match the parts that most likely go together.**

	Adjective	Noun	Adjective phrase
a	chocolate	groups	from the fire
b	birthday	sparks	decorated with icing
c	red	cakes	with lots of presents
d	exciting	plans	of happy people
e	large	parties	for the future

8 **In each sentence, underline the adjective phrase.**

a The children were very excited this morning.

b That shop sells beautiful, handmade fans.

c The children have eaten far too much cake.

d Priya is the girl in the brightly coloured dress.

e Priya and Adi were exactly the same age.

LESSON 186

Water

Word Study

We can often use clues in the text to help us work out the meaning of words we do not understand.

Read the passage.

Put a box around the area rivers collect water from.

Circle the base word of *catchment*.

Most of the water we use comes from rivers, lakes or dams.

A river starts from melting ice, rainfall or from a lake, and grows as streams in its catchment area join it.

An important source of fresh water is ground water. The water collects above a layer of rock that is too dense to allow it to flow through. People dig wells to bring this water to the surface again. Around the world, ground water is the most accessible source of fresh water — about 1.5 billion people use it for their drinking water.

Colour how people bring ground water to the surface.

Underline why so many people use ground water.

Circle the correct answers.

1. What is a catchment area? It is an area where water...
   - a flows away.
   - b collects.
   - c dries up.
   - d enters the ocean.
2. What is the **clue** to question 1's answer?
   - a The word *melting* suggests that the water vanishes.
   - b The word *grows* shows that the river gets bigger.
   - c The word *stream* means *to flow*.
   - d The base word of *catchment* is *catch*, which means *to hold on to*.
3. What does the word *accessible* mean?
   - a can be easily reached
   - b unfit for use
   - c happens by chance
   - d fashionable
4. Which group of words is the **clue** to question 3's answer?
   - a The water collects above a layer of rock
   - b too dense to allow it to flow through
   - c about 1.5 billion people use it for their drinking water
   - d grows as streams in its catchment area join it

AC9E6LY05 Use comprehension strategies such as connecting to build literal and inferred meaning

Read the passage.

In paragraph 1, circle the word that helps to explain what *purified* means.

In paragraph 2, **highlight** the word that refers to things in the water that are harmful.

In paragraph 2, **colour** the word that means *to clot* or *thicken*.

Drinking water is water that is safe for people to drink and to use for cooking, washing and bathing. Water is cleaned and purified before it is ready to drink.

Water is pumped from a river, lake or dam into a tank. A chemical called alum is added to the water so that impurities coagulate into small particles called flocs.

The water is then transferred into a sedimentation tank. The flocs attract dirt and sink to the bottom as sediment. The clear water above the sediment is pumped to the next stage, filtration.

In paragraph 3, underline the word that refers to solid material at the bottom of a liquid.

In paragraph 3, put a box around the word that refers to the process of removing unwanted material.

Explain what the following words mean.

5 Use the clues in the passage and the boxes to help you.

a purified ______________________________

____

b impurities ______________________________

____

c coagulate ______________________________

____

d sediment ______________________________

____

e filtration ______________________________

____

LESSON 187

What's Cooking?

Finding the Main Idea and Supporting Details

To discover what a text is about, you need to look for the main idea or key point. Facts and details in the text can help you find the main idea.

Read the passage.

Highlight who Marc-Antoine Careme was.

Colour the words that suggest that Careme was a very creative chef.

Underline who Careme cooked for.

Marc-Antoine Careme (1784–1833) was considered the master of French cooking, creating dishes that often looked more like sculptures. He cooked for royalty and the rich and famous. His cuisine was the talk of Europe.

Via his travels, Careme introduced to France such delicacies as caviar (unfertilised fish eggs) and *pashka* (a creamy Russian cheesecake).

While in England, he produced a jellied custard set in a crown of ladyfingers (long, thin biscuits). He named it the Charlotte Russe — a pastry still baked today.

Careme also prepared massive feasts. At one military festival, he served 10 000 guests from a menu that required 6 cows, 75 calves, 250 sheep, 8000 turkeys, 2000 chickens, 1000 partridges, 500 hams and 2000 fish.

Highlight the delicacies Careme introduced to France.

Put a box around the dish Careme produced while in England.

Circle the word that describes the feasts.

Circle the correct answers.

1. What is the passage **mainly** about?
   - a the achievements of Marc-Antoine Careme
   - b the type of food people ate 200 years ago
   - c unusual delicacies
   - d cooking for large numbers of people

2. Which **three details** support the **main idea**?
   - a The Charlotte Russe is a pastry that is still baked today.
   - b Careme created dishes that often looked more like sculptures.
   - c Careme produced a jellied custard.
   - d Careme prepared massive feasts.
   - e *Pashka* is a creamy Russian cheesecake.
   - f Ladyfingers are a delicacy.
   - g Careme lived from 1784-1833.

AC9E6LY05 Use comprehension strategies such as connecting and summarising to build literal and inferred meaning

Read the passage.

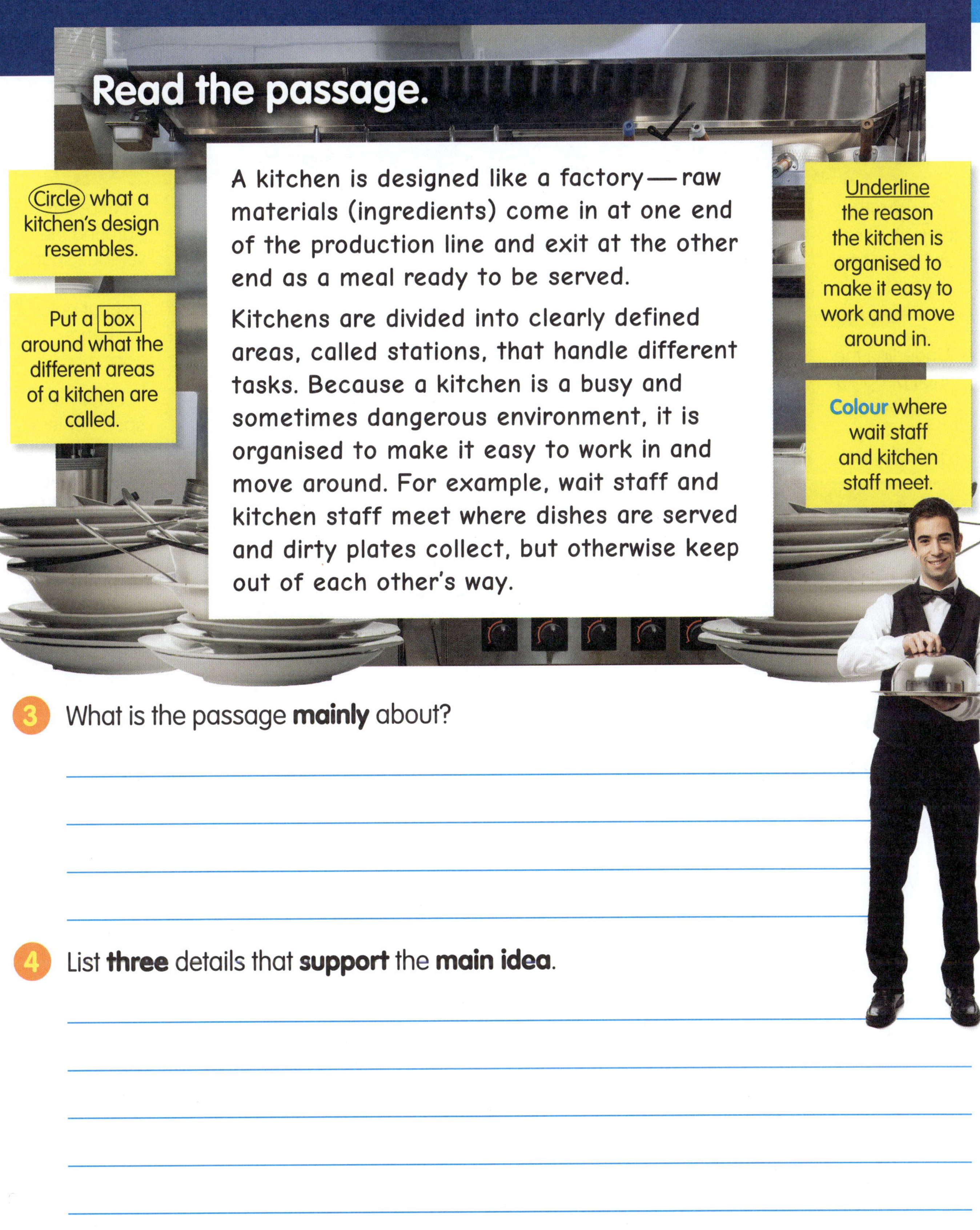

A kitchen is designed like a factory — raw materials (ingredients) come in at one end of the production line and exit at the other end as a meal ready to be served.

Kitchens are divided into clearly defined areas, called stations, that handle different tasks. Because a kitchen is a busy and sometimes dangerous environment, it is organised to make it easy to work in and move around. For example, wait staff and kitchen staff meet where dishes are served and dirty plates collect, but otherwise keep out of each other's way.

3 What is the passage **mainly** about?

4 List **three** details that **support** the **main idea**.

LESSON 188

Endangered Animals

Point of View

To identify the author's point of view in a non-fiction text, we need to look at his or her choice of words and details. These will help to reveal the author's beliefs, personal judgements or attitudes towards the subject.

Read the passage.

Circle what the Inuit people use polar bear fur for.

Underline the Inuit people's reasons for killing polar bears.

Polar bears live mainly on ice floes in the Arctic. They are not endangered now, but they are considered at risk and in need of conservation.

Polar bears have been hunted for thousands of years by the native Inuit people who share their habitat. Inuit people use polar bear fur for clothing, and the meat and fat for food. They kill only what they need to survive.

Sport hunters began using aircraft and motor boats to hunt polar bears. As a result, bear numbers have declined.

Put a box around the vehicles sport hunters use to hunt polar bears.

Colour how sport hunters have affected polar bear numbers.

Circle the correct answers.

1. What is the author's **attitude** towards the Inuit people's reason for hunting polar bears?
   - a hostile
   - b sympathetic
   - c accusatory
   - d undecided
2. Which group of words is the best **clue** to question 1's answer?
   - a hunted for thousands of years
   - b share their habitat
   - c use polar bear fur
   - d only what they need to survive
3. What is the author's **attitude** towards the sport hunters' reason for hunting polar bears?
   - a disapproving
   - b admiring
   - c respectful
   - d tolerant
4. What is the **clue** to question 3's answer? The author …
   - a describes how sport hunters kill polar bears.
   - b mentions how often sport hunters kill polar bears.
   - c describes the sport hunters' aircraft and motor boats.
   - d mentions that sport hunters are responsible for the decline in bear numbers.

AC9E6LY05 Use comprehension strategies such as questioning to build inferred meaning

Read the passage.

Highlight the rhetorical question.

Underline how closely related chimpanzees and humans are.

In the last 500 years, humans have forced 844 species to extinction. Will we ever stop?

Chimpanzees are one of the species in danger. They are our closest relative in the animal world, sharing an estimated 98 percent of our genes. Chimpanzees are highly intelligent and show emotions like happiness and sadness, fear and love. Yet, humans threaten their future.

Urgent action is necessary to protect the remaining chimpanzee populations.

Put a box around four words that show how strongly the author feels about the need to save the chimpanzees.

Circle the qualities and emotions chimpanzees share with humans.

5. How does the author **feel** about the role humans have played in the destruction of so many animal species? Support your answer with a quote from the passage.

6. Explain how the author uses language to **persuade** us of the need to protect chimpanzees.

7. How does the author **feel** about the need to protect chimpanzees? Support your answer with a quote.

LESSON 189

Proceed with Caution

Making Connections

Linking a text to other texts you have read is a great way to build understanding. Look for key words and phrases in the texts to make the connections.

Read the passages.

Text 1

The site plan of the new development on the city's edge has sparked a firestorm of debate. The plan includes a staggering number of standard office, retail and apartment buildings, which seem to grow taller with every new glossy brochure that the developer produces. But it is not like the city is filled with beautiful architecture that this new waterfront development will somehow "spoil".

In both texts, underline the sentence that contains the word *debate.*

In both texts, **highlight** the words that describe the buildings planned for the new development.

In both texts, **colour** the words that refer to the location of the new development.

Text 2

A proposal to build 20-storey office and apartment towers across a section of the harbour has become a topic of heated debate. On the one hand, there are those who argue that the city can expand in one direction only—upwards. Others, however, believe that too many tall buildings along the water's edge will spoil the look and feel of the city's greatest asset—its beautiful, meandering waterway.

1 Write down whether the following information appears in **both** of the texts, or just **one** of the texts.

a The new development is taking place on the waterfront. ____________

b The new development will consist of a large number of tall buildings. ____________

c The developers have outlined their plans in a number of glossy brochures. ____________

d The new development has led to fierce arguments between different groups of people. ____________

e The buildings in the city are generally not beautiful. ____________

f The city's greatest attraction is its harbour. ____________

g The new development is not likely to spoil the look of the city. ____________

AC9E6LY05 Use comprehension strategies to connect and compare content from a variety of sources

Read the passages.

Text 1

We do have a beautiful city, but it relies heavily on its natural charms, rather than what we've built in it. If we are to see our city grow and change, let's be brave and embrace what the world's best architects are offering. If we are not careful, this development could turn into yet another maze of concrete canyons which rarely see sunshine. Loudly expressed public opinion could make all the difference.

In both texts, **highlight** the sentences that express the authors' concerns about what the new development could become.

In both texts, underline the sentences that show what the authors think ordinary citizens should be doing.

Text 2

The plans for the new development on the waterfront fill me with dismay. Are our city planners really going to allow this section of the harbour to become just another concrete jungle? Surely there are architects out there who can come up with more creative and exciting plans for the area!

I urge those of you who feel as I do to stand up and make your voices heard!

2 What do the authors of both passages feel about the plans for the new development? Support your answer with quotes from the passages.

___

___

___

___

3 What suggestions do the authors of both passages put forward to make sure that the new development does not become just another series of dull grey buildings?

___

___

___

___

___

___

LESSON 190

Base on the Moon

Fact or Opinion?

A fact is a statement that can be proved to be true; for example: A spider has eight legs. An opinion is a statement that expresses a belief or feeling; for example: Spiders are ugly.

Read the passage.

In paragraph 1, **highlight** the fact.

In paragraph 1, underline the opinion.

In paragraph 2, **highlight** two facts about how space settlements must be constructed.

Space settlements are enclosed areas in orbit. Scientists believe that people will live in these settlements sometime in the future.

Space settlements could be in the shape of a sphere, cylinder or even a doughnut, but they must be airtight, so they maintain air pressure and a breathable atmosphere. They must also rotate in order to create artificial gravity.

Space settlements need constant sunlight to produce solar power. They also need some sort of barrier to protect them from the Sun's radiation. On Earth, our atmosphere provides this protection. Later settlements may decide to leave our solar system, but they will still need protection from the radiation of other stars.

In paragraph 3, **highlight** a fact about future space settlements need for protection from the sun.

In paragraph 3, underline an opinion about what later settlements may do.

1 Are the following statements facts, or opinions? Write **F** next to the facts, and **O** next to the opinions.

- **a** Space settlements are enclosed areas in orbit. ______
- **b** Scientists believe that people will live in these settlements sometime in the future. ______
- **c** Space settlements must be airtight. ______
- **d** Space settlements need to maintain air pressure and a breathable atmosphere. ______
- **e** Space settlements must rotate in order to create artificial gravity. ______
- **f** Space settlements need constant sunlight to produce solar power. ______
- **g** On Earth, our atmosphere protects us from the Sun's radiation. ______
- **h** Later settlements may decide to leave our solar system. ______

AC9E6LY05 Use comprehension strategies such as questioning to build literal and inferred meaning

Read the passage.

Highlight an opinion about what people living in space may want.

Colour NASA's opinion on the possibility of building settlements in space.

People living in space may still want regular contact and visits with Earth. Therefore, spacecraft launches from both Earth and the settlement will need to be cheap. An environmentally-safe method of launching craft from Earth needs to be invented, due to the risk to the Earth's atmosphere from a large number of launches.

NASA has studied the possibility of building space settlements in orbit. They believe it is possible, as plenty of the necessary materials are available on the Moon or on asteroids. The sun could supply the necessary energy. NASA believes no new scientific breakthroughs are necessary, but lots of engineering would be required.

Circle where materials and energy for future settlements in space could come from.

Highlight NASA's opinion about what needs to be done before settlements in space are possible.

2 Write down an **opinion** from paragraph 1.

3 On what **fact** is the need to invent an environmentally-safe method of launching craft from Earth based?

4 What is NASA's **opinion** about the possibility of people living in space?

5 On what **fact** has NASA based its **opinion** about the possibility of people living in space?

GRAMMAR LESSON 2

Dashes and Semi-colons

Dashes (—) can be used in place of **commas (,)** and **colons (:)**. They separate information in sentences. For example: **There are three things I love to do—swim, surf and ride my bike.**

Semi-colons (;) can be used to join **clauses**. The clauses are usually of equal importance. For example: **I like dogs; my sister prefers cats.**

Read the extract.

In this sentence, circle the **dash** and underline the parts of an atom.

In this sentence, put a box around the **dashes** and **highlight** the part of the atom that forms the nucleus.

In this sentence, circle the **semi-colon** and **colour** the clauses it separates.

In this sentence, put a box around the **dash** and underline the information that follows it.

The Atom

Everything in the world is made up of atoms. They are the main building blocks of matter.

Atoms are made up of three parts—neutrons, protons and electrons. The nucleus—the centre of the atom—is made from neutrons and protons. The electrons orbit the nucleus, just like the planets orbit our sun.

Protons have a positive electrical charge; electrons have a negative charge.

When a positive electrical charge comes into contact with a negative charge, they are attracted to each other. This is what happens with electrons and protons. Alternatively, two things with the same electrical charge repel each other. An atom normally has the same number of protons and electrons—their opposite electrical charges balance each other and make the atom stable.

Circle the correct answers.

In each sentence, which punctuation can replace the colon?

1. The nucleus is the centre of the atom and is made from two parts: neutrons and protons.
   a ; **b** ? **c** . **d** —

2. Matter comes in three main forms: solid, liquid and gas.
   a ; **b** — **c** . **d** !

Which punctuation can replace the full stop to join the following pairs of sentences?

3. Some atoms have too many electrons. Some atoms are short of electrons.
   a ! **b** ? **c** . **d** ;

4. Salt is made up of sodium and chlorine. Sugar is made up of carbon, hydrogen and oxygen.
   a ; **b** ? **c** . **d** !

5. Atoms are tiny particles. It takes millions of them to make up a single grain of sand.
   a ! **b** ; **c** . **d** ?

AC9E6LA03 Explain how authors use text structures and language features

6 **In each sentence, insert a ∧ to show where a dash is needed.**

- **a** Atoms last a long time in most cases forever.
- **b** The hydrogen atom is unique it has a single proton and no neutrons in its nucleus.
- **c** There are two particles that are even smaller than atoms quarks and neutrinos.
- **d** There are six types of quarks up, down, top, bottom, charm and strange.
- **e** All matter is composed of atoms they are the building blocks of the universe.
- **f** Electrons can move in any direction upwards, downwards or sideways.

7 **Rewrite the following sentences by replacing the conjunction with a semi-colon.**

- **a** Solids are made of densely packed atoms, while atoms have gases that are spread out.

  ____

  ____

- **b** The electron always has a negative charge, and the proton always has a positive charge.

  ____

  ____

- **c** A normal atom has a neutral charge because it has equal numbers of positive and negative charges.

  ____

  ____

- **d** Neutrons aren't positive or negative, so they have a neutral charge.

  ____

  ____

- **e** Ice becomes water when it is heated, and water becomes ice when it is cooled to 0° Celsius or lower.

  ____

  ____

ASSESSMENT 1:

Computer Annihilation

Lexile: 960L

The year is 2040 and warfare is raging across the globe. It's not one country fighting against another, or even one religious group trying to destroy another. This is warfare like the world has never seen before. This is humans against machines.

Back in 2038—what seems like ages ago—the Athan Computer Group (or ACG) perfected a revolutionary new chip that enabled computers to learn in the same way humans do. And learn they did, at an incomprehensible rate. Not only did they learn what ACG was about, but they linked into the worldwide web of the internet and, in no time at all, computers all over the world were sharing and adding to their knowledge. Soon their abilities outstripped those of their human creators.

Computers ended up controlling everything, from banking and finance to education, medicine and communication. They even controlled defence. But the real trouble started on 29 February 2040 when, inexplicably, computers all over the world started to shut down. Transport, banks, the stock market, hospitals and businesses all came to a standstill.

Programmers and technicians tried their best to rectify the problem, but they were unsuccessful. In frustration, one technician picked up a monitor and smashed it so hard against a wall that it broke into a thousand pieces. Unfortunately, computers had just learned a new behaviour—revenge, and it wasn't long before they began attacking humans and, of course, humans were fighting back.

Now it is all-out war as humans from all parts of the globe are united—for the first time ever—in an effort to stop the machines. Luckily the nuclear warheads were removed under a treaty signed by all countries; otherwise there would no longer be a world to fight over. But those warheads are in storage! Who monitors and controls the storage? Noooo ...

Circle the correct answer for each question.

1 Where is the war being fought? **LITERAL**

- **a** in the Northern Hemisphere
- **b** all over the world
- **c** in computer laboratories
- **d** in Europe and America

2 What made it possible for computers to learn so quickly? LITERAL

a the revolutionary new chip
b the education system
c information from ACG
d the internet

3 Inexplicably, computers started to shut down. This means they started to shut down … VOCABULARY

a without warning.
b at different times.
c in a way that could not be explained.
d in an unusual way.

4 What is the most likely reason the computers started to shut down? CRITICAL

a to recharge their batteries
b to cause chaos for humans
c to update their software
d to have a rest

5 What positive outcome did the war have for humans? Humans … INFERENTIAL

a started to work together.
b discovered new weapons.
c became less aggressive.
d no longer needed computers.

6 What is a treaty? VOCABULARY

a an agreement between computers
b a computer program
c an agreement between countries
d a storage facility

7 Who has access to the nuclear warheads? INFERENTIAL

a the humans
b the computers
c certain countries only
d no one

8 What type of story is this? CRITICAL

a romance
b horror
c science fiction
d crime

9 Why were computers able to imitate human behaviour? LITERAL

____

____

10 What could happen if the computers used nuclear warheads against the humans? INFERENTIAL

____

____

LESSON 191

Teacher's Pet

Summarising

A summary is a shortened version of the original text. To summarise a text, you need to look for the points and details that contain the most important information.

Read the passage.

Put a box around what the class gave Mr Sams.

Underline what the principal told the class.

Circle the word that suggests that Andy got out of bed unwillingly.

Colour what Andy's mum was doing.

Highlight what Andy's mum said to him.

On the Friday before he left, we gave Mr Sams a surprise farewell party. It wasn't really a surprise because he saw us carrying the party things to school.

It was almost time to go when the principal, Mr Jones, came into our classroom to tell us a new teacher would start on Monday.

On Monday morning, I dragged myself out of bed again. "Another fun day," I thought, wishing I could change places with my older brother, Joel.

"You might get a nice surprise, Andy," Mum said as she packed my lunch. "You might even like this new teacher."

Circle the correct answers.

1. Which sentence better **summarises** paragraph 1?
   - a The party the class gave Mr Sams wasn't really a surprise.
   - b On the Friday before he left, the class gave Mr Sams a farewell party.
2. Which sentence better **sums up** what happens in paragraph 2?
   - a The principal told them a new teacher would start on Monday.
   - b Mr Jones, the principal, came to their classroom to make an announcement.
3. Which sentence provides the best **summary** of paragraph 3?
   - a On Monday, Andy wished he could change places with Joel.
   - b On Monday, Andy dragged himself out of bed.
   - c On Monday, Andy didn't feel like going to school.
4. Which sentence better **summarises** paragraph 4?
   - a Andy's mum packed his lunch, so he had to go to school.
   - b Andy's mum said he might like the new teacher.

AC9E6LY05 Use comprehension strategies such as summarising to build inferred meaning

Read the passage.

Highlight what Andy did the next morning.

Underline the reason Andy did not give the roses to Miss Thompson in the parking lot.

Circle where Andy put the roses.

The next morning I gathered a big armful of roses from Mum's garden. I wrapped them in some cellophane left over from my birthday.

I was going to give them to Miss Thompson in the parking lot, but I changed my mind at the last minute. What if someone saw me? I'd look like a dork. Instead, I slipped into the classroom before the bell rang and put them on her desk.

When Miss Thompson saw them, she couldn't have looked happier. "What a beautiful bunch of roses!" she exclaimed. "Someone in this class must have guessed that they are my favourite flower. I love them! Who was the kind person who brought them in?"

Everybody looked around the room. Of course nobody answered. I wanted to say it was me, but I couldn't. Not in front of everyone!

Colour the words that describe the look on Miss Thompson's face when she saw the roses.

Put a box around the sentence that suggests that Andy was too embarrassed to say he had brought the roses.

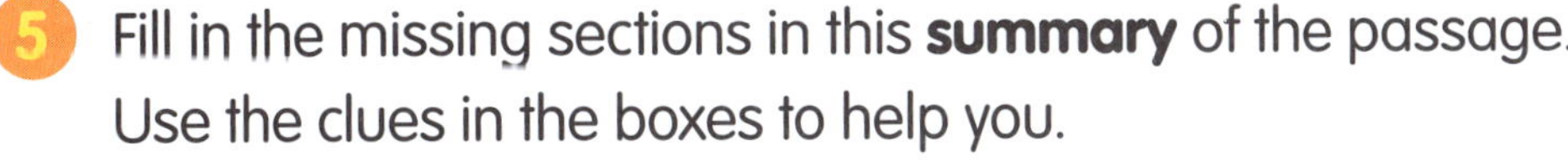

5 Fill in the missing sections in this **summary** of the passage. Use the clues in the boxes to help you.

a The next morning Andy ______________________________ .

b He put them ______________________________ .

c Miss Thompson was ______________________________ .

d She wanted to know ______________________________ .

e Andy was too embarrassed ______________________________ .

The Plight of E. Hammond

Finding Facts and Information

To find facts and information in a text, we usually ask the questions **Who? What? Where?** or **When?** The answers can be clearly seen in the text.

Read the passage.

Highlight the names of the children in the Hammond family.

Circle Elizabeth Hammond's age.

Put a box around the words that describe James.

Elizabeth Hammond has a busy life. Much busier than the average eleven-year-old. Elizabeth has a brother, James, aged eight — 'a space-occupying lesion'; another brother aged five, called Ted — 'sweet but useless'; twin sisters Harriet and Lucy, aged twenty-two months — 'still in nappies'; and a father called Jim who spends all day in the attic, except for mealtimes — 'trying to write a bestseller'. That is the Hammond family.

Underline the name of the sweet but useless child.

Colour the place where Jim spends most of the day.

Highlight what Jim does in the attic.

Circle the correct answers.

1. **How many** children are there in the Hammond family?
   a five b four c six d three

2. **Who** is the oldest child in the Hammond family?
   a Jim b James c Elizabeth d Ted

3. **Which** child is sweet but useless?
   a Lucy b Ted c James d Harriet

4. **Where** does Jim spend most of his time?
   a in his study b at work c in his bedroom d in the attic

5. **What** does Jim do all day?
   a writes articles for magazines b makes phone calls
   c works on his book d writes computer programs

AC9E6LY05 Use comprehension strategies such as questioning to build literal meaning

Read the passage.

Highlight the reason Elizabeth cannot see her knees.

Circle where Heather Shambles had put the dirty laundry.

Put a box around what Elizabeth did when she sat amongst the bubbles.

Underline the words Heather Shambles speaks.

Colour what Elizabeth notices when she finally stops laughing.

Elizabeth can't see her knees in the mountain of bubbles and wet clothes. She looks at Heather Shambles and says quietly, "You put the dirty laundry in the dishwasher."

Elizabeth hears her voice trembling. In this crazy moment she wonders whether to cry or shout. Instead, she sits down amongst the bubbles and laughs.

"At least I didn't put the plates in the washing machine," mutters Heather Shambles.

Elizabeth rolls around the kitchen floor, laughing and squealing and kicking her feet in the air. Finally, when she lies quite still, she notices everyone is staring at her. Heather Shambles, Ted, Harriet, Lucy, James— and her father.

6 **What** stops Elizabeth from seeing her knees?

7 **Where** did Heather Shambles put the dirty laundry?

8 **What** does Elizabeth do when she realises what Heather Shambles has done?

9 **Who** else is in the kitchen with Elizabeth?

LESSON 193

The Black Velvet Band

Identifying Audience and Purpose

To identify the author's purpose in writing a text, it helps to work out who the text was written for. The language the author uses will show what his or her purpose is—to inform, persuade, instruct, or entertain.

Read the passage.

Circle the word that is similar in meaning to *walking*.

Highlight the old-fashioned word for a young woman.

Colour why the narrator was put in prison.

As I went strolling one evening,
Not meaning to go very far,
I spied a pretty young damsel,
Parading her wares at an inn,
A watch she took from a customer,
And she slipped it right in my hand,
And the law came and put me in prison,
Bad luck to her black velvet band.

Chorus

Her eyes shone like the diamonds,
You'd think she was Queen of the land,
And her hair hung over her shoulder,
Tied up with a black velvet band.

Put a box around the words that rhyme with *band*.

Circle the word that shows which part of the text is meant to be repeated after each verse.

Underline an example of a simile.

Circle the correct answers.

1. What type of text is this? Choose the best answer.
   - a a narrative
   - b a song
   - c a poem
   - d a report
2. Which word is the **clue** to question 1's answer?
   - a damsel
   - b Queen
   - c Chorus
   - d band
3. Who is the intended **audience** for this text?
   - a the general public
   - b musicians
   - c innkeepers
   - d lawyers
4. What gives the text its musical quality?
   - a the vivid imagery
   - b the repetition of words
   - c the mournful tone
   - d the rhyme and rhythm
5. What is the main **purpose** of the text?
   - a to persuade
   - b to entertain
   - c to inform
   - d to warn

AC9E6LY03 Analyse how text structures and language features work together to meet the purpose of a text

Read the passage.

In line 1, **highlight** an example of alliteration.

Underline the sentence the judge handed down to the narrator.

Next morning before judge and jury,
For trial I had to appear,

And the judge said "Me fine young fellow
The case against you is quite clear,
For seven long years is your sentence,
You're going to Van Diemen's Land,
Away from your friends and relations,
To follow the black velvet band."

Chorus

Her eyes shone like the diamonds,
You'd think she was Queen of the land,
And her hair hung over her shoulder,
Tied up with a black velvet band.

Colour the line that indicates that the judge had no doubt that the narrator was guilty.

Put boxes around the words that rhyme in lines 2 and 4.

6 What are the most likely reasons someone wrote this song?

7 Rewrite the song as a narrative. Include information from both passages in your story.

LESSON 194

Sunglasses

Figurative Language

Alliteration repeats consonant sounds. **Onomatopoeia** imitates sounds. **Similes** compare one thing to something unlike itself by using the words *like* or *as*. **Metaphors** make a more direct comparison. They do not contain the words *like* or *as*. **Personification** is a type of metaphor that gives animals and objects human qualities.

Read the passage.

Circle the alliteration in stanza 1.

Highlight the simile in stanza 2.

Put a box around the alliteration in stanza 2.

I look cool
in these glasses
in the mirror
I am tinted
smooth
slick

Natalie said
my old glasses
made me look like
a bogong moth
big black orbs
instead of eyes

Circle the correct answers.

1. What **figure of speech** is *smooth / slick*?
   a a simile b a metaphor c onomatopoeia d alliteration
2. What is the **clue** to question 1's answer?
   a Consonant sounds are repeated.
   b The words imitate sounds.
   c The poet gives the mirror human qualities.
   d The poet uses the word *like*.
3. Which of the following **figures of speech** occurs in stanza 2?
   a personification b onomatopoeia c a metaphor d a simile
4. What is the **clue** to question 3's answer?
   a The poet uses the word *like*.
   b Consonant sounds are repeated.
   c The words imitate sounds.
   d The poet gives the moth human qualities.

AC9E6LA08 Identify authors' use of vivid, emotive vocabulary, such as metaphors, similes, personification, idioms, imagery and hyperbole

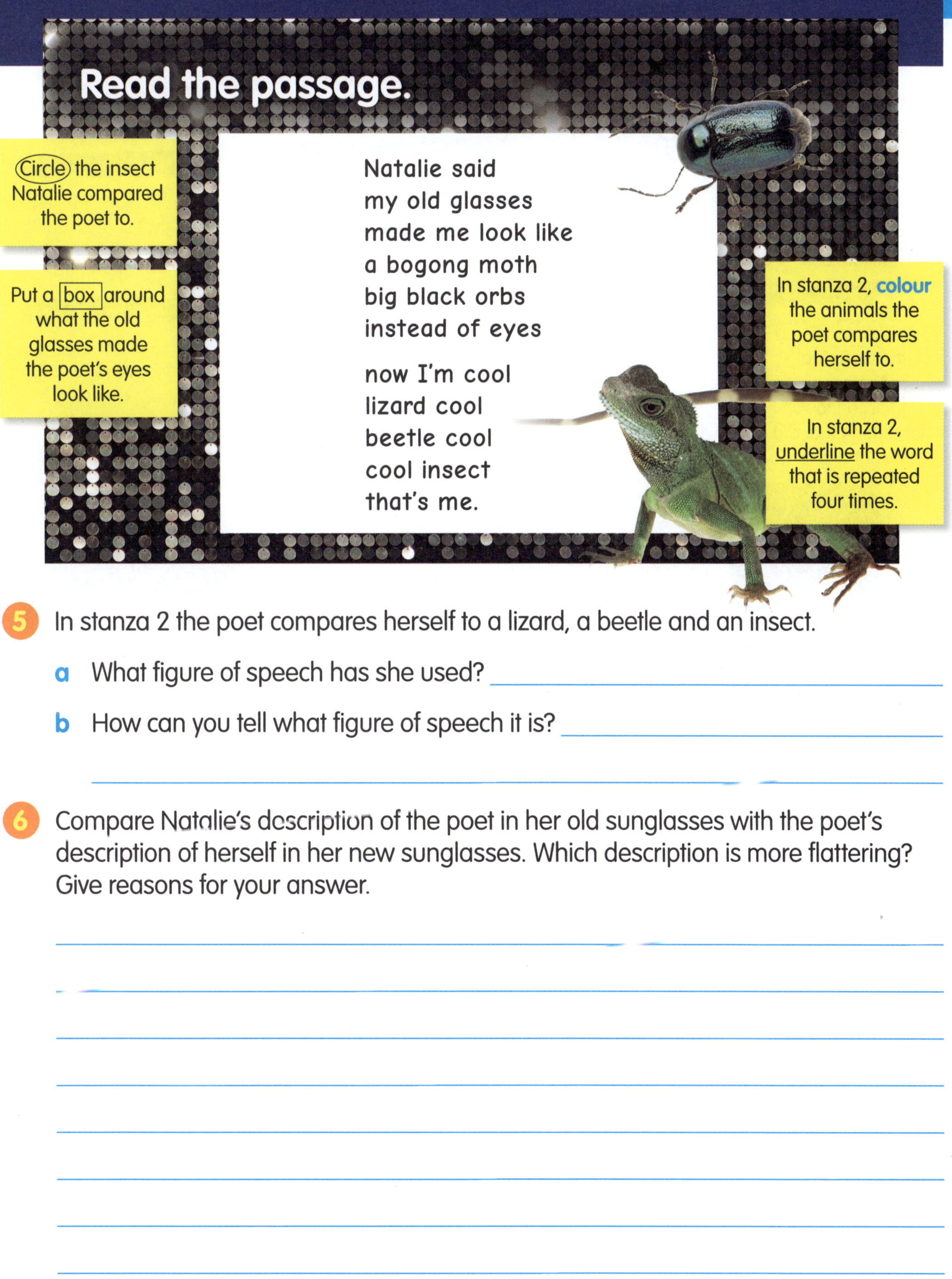

Read the passage.

Circle the insect Natalie compared the poet to.

Put a box around what the old glasses made the poet's eyes look like.

Natalie said
my old glasses
made me look like
a bogong moth
big black orbs
instead of eyes

now I'm cool
lizard cool
beetle cool
cool insect
that's me.

In stanza 2, **colour** the animals the poet compares herself to.

In stanza 2, underline the word that is repeated four times.

5 In stanza 2 the poet compares herself to a lizard, a beetle and an insect.

a What figure of speech has she used? ______________________

b How can you tell what figure of speech it is? ______________________

____

6 Compare Natalie's description of the poet in her old sunglasses with the poet's description of herself in her new sunglasses. Which description is more flattering? Give reasons for your answer.

____

____

____

____

____

____

____

____

LESSON 195

Why Parrots Only Repeat What People Say

Word Study

To help us understand how authors shape our view of a subject, we need to look at their choice of words. Words such as *sweet* and *innocent* have a positive connotation, while *glum* and *guilty* have a negative connotation.

Read the passage.

Circle the adjective that describes the lorikeet.

Put a box around the word that indicates that the man took something that did not belong to him.

A long time ago, lorikeets not only repeated what a person said, they also spoke their own thoughts.

That was until a man who owned a magnificent lorikeet stole his neighbour's water buffalo. When the neighbour asked if the man knew anything about it, he lied and said, "I have no idea."

But the lorikeet knew the truth. It called out, "Brrk! Master stole it! Master killed it! Master ate part and hid the rest in the rice bins. Brrk!"

Colour the verb that shows that the man did not tell the truth.

Underline the word that is similar in meaning to *concealed*.

Circle the correct answers.

1. Which word creates a **positive** impression of the lorikeet?
   - a repeated
   - b spoke
   - c magnificent
   - d owned

2. In paragraph 2, which two words create a **negative** impression of the man?
   - a neighbour
   - b idea
   - c lorikeet
   - d stole
   - e asked
   - f lied

3. In paragraph 3, which word is most closely associated with the lorikeet?
   - a truth
   - b stole
   - c killed
   - d ate

4. In the following pairs, which word has the more **negative** connotation?
   - a took / stole
   - b hid / put
   - c ate / gobbled

5. Which of these words has the **most positive** connotation?
   - a attractive
   - b cute
   - c beautiful
   - d pleasing

AC9E6LA08 Identify authors' use of vivid, emotive vocabulary

Read the passage.

Circle the adjective that describes the man.

Put a box around the word that describes the parrot's colours.

Underline the lorikeet's warning to the parrot.

The guilty man went free. He left the bird, wanting never to see it again. The lorikeet flew back to the jungle, where it met a new bird, the parrot. The lorikeet looked at the parrot's wonderful colours and knew that, one day, man would want it for a pet. The lorikeet warned the parrot, "Brrt! Do not speak your own mind to people! You will get into a lot of trouble. Repeat only what they say. They love to hear their own thoughts."

Today, the parrot remembers the lorikeet's warning, and this is why it only repeats what people say.

6 Which word in the passage gives the most **negative** impression of the man?

7 Which actions of the man add to our **negative** impression of him?

8 Which words paint a **positive** image of the parrot?

9 Which word suggests that the parrot could one day experience problems if it speaks its own mind to people?

10 Which sentence suggests that people have a high opinion of themselves?

GRAMMAR LESSON 3

Perfect Continuous Tense

The **present perfect continuous tense** is formed by placing the auxiliary verbs **have been** or **has been** before the main verb. For example: **They have been riding their bikes**. The **past perfect continuous tense** is formed by placing the auxiliary verbs **had been** before the main verb. For example: **She had been waiting for hours when the train finally arrived.**

Read the extract.

Tom's Ambition

Tom had ambition. He wanted to be Prime Minister when he grew up.

In this paragraph, underline the **past perfect tense** verb.

Another thing Tom wanted was a fish. That was why he was at the pet shop staring at the fish tanks. He had been saving his pocket money for weeks and now he finally had enough.

In this paragraph, highlight two **past perfect tense** verbs.

But while Tom had been staring at the fish, a ferret had been eyeing him. Now it tried to get his attention. "Psst!" it said.

Tom turned around, but no-one was there.

"What's the matter with you, Kid?" said the ferret. "You must have bananas in your ears. Can't you hear when someone is talking to you?"

The ferret was in a cage near Tom. It was standing on its hind legs, with its paws resting on the bars of its cage. It was looking straight at Tom with beady little eyes.

Circle the correct answers.

Which word correctly completes each sentence?

1 Tom _____ been telling everyone he wants to be Prime Minister.

a have b is c are d has

2 Tom _____ been looking at the fish when the ferret spoke to him.

a has b have c had d were

3 The fish _____ been investigating the new structure in their tank.

a have b has c are d were

4 The ferret has been _____ in a cage for months.

a live b living c lived

5 The ferret had been _____ Tom all the time.

a watch b watched c watching

AC9E6LA06 Understand how ideas can be expanded and sharpened

6 **Complete each sentence with a suitable verb.**

a The fish have been ______________________ in circles.

b The fish had not been ______________________ their food.

c Water has been ______________________ from the fish tank.

d Tom has been ______________________ to the pet shop every day this week.

e Tom had been ______________________ his pocket money to buy a fish.

f We have been ______________________ all morning for our fish tank to arrive.

7 **In each sentence, underline the incorrect verb and write it correctly.**

a He have been working in the pet shop since the beginning of the year. ______________

b The ferret has been saying something when the pet shop owner looked up. ______________

c I has been talking to Tom's ferret all morning and he's very funny. ______________

d The ferret was bored because it have been living in a cage for months. ______________

e The ferret have been looking for someone to rescue it from the cage. ______________

8 **In each sentence, write the verb in brackets in the present continuous tense.**

a Tom (find) ______________________ information on fish.

b The ferret (try) ______________________ to get Tom's attention.

c Lately, the pet shop (sell) ______________________ more fish.

d Tom's friends (help) ______________________ him set up his fish tank.

e Tom (mean) ______________________ to clean the fish tank.

f Tom (listen) ______________________ to the ferret for the last ten minutes.

LESSON 196

Space Stations

Compare and Contrast

When we compare and contrast information, we look for the similarities and differences between details in the text.

Read the passage.

Circle the type of gravity that is found in orbit.

Put a box around the words that describe the food on a space station.

Highlight why knives, forks and spoons don't float away on a space station.

There is very little gravity in orbit, so it is known as microgravity. This means things are done differently from the way they are done on Earth.

Food is mainly dehydrated or heat-stabilised. Drinks are also dehydrated. Once food has been rehydrated and heated, astronauts eat the food on magnetic trays. The magnetic tray means that the knives, forks and spoons stick to the trays and don't float away. A straw is used for drinks.

Astronauts sleep in sleeping bags attached to the walls of the station. They zip themselves in so they don't float out of the bag while asleep.

Underline where people on a space station sleep.

Colour the reason people on a space station have to zip themselves into their sleeping bags.

Circle the correct answers.

1. How is living on a space station **similar** to living on Earth? In both places, people …
   - a can float to the ceiling.
   - b have a view of Earth.
   - c go on space walks.
   - d eat, drink and sleep.
2. How is the food on a space station **different** from food on Earth? On a space station, the food is mainly …
   - a fresh.
   - b frozen.
   - c dehydrated.
   - d raw.
3. How is eating food on a space station **different** from eating food on Earth? On a space station, food is served on …
   - a paper plates.
   - b magnetic trays.
   - c plastic trays.
   - d wooden plates.
4. How is sleeping on a space station **different** from sleeping on Earth? On a space station, people sleep …
   - a in zipped-up sleeping bags.
   - b on bunk beds.
   - c on mattresses on the floor.
   - d attached to a wall.

AC9E6LY05 Use comprehension strategies to connect and compare content

Read the passage.

Circle what people have already done on the Moon.

Underline what the future plans for the Moon are.

Highlight how gravity on the Moon is different from gravity on Earth.

Although people have already walked on the Moon, there are plans for further exploration, and even a permanent settlement, on the Moon.

Some people believe that the Moon is a ready-made space station. Further exploration of space could occur from a Moon base. As there is less gravity, spacecraft would need less energy to take off from the Moon than they do from Earth.

Water ice has been discovered at the Moon's poles. This could be melted for drinking water, and broken down into oxygen for breathing and hydrogen for nuclear fuel.

The south pole of the Moon is an ideal position for a base. This site can provide water ice. There is also a mountain which receives almost continuous sunlight. If solar panels were installed, a Moon base could use solar energy.

Put a box around a substance that occurs on both Earth and the Moon.

Colour the gas that humans need to survive.

Circle the type of light that occurs on both Earth and the Moon.

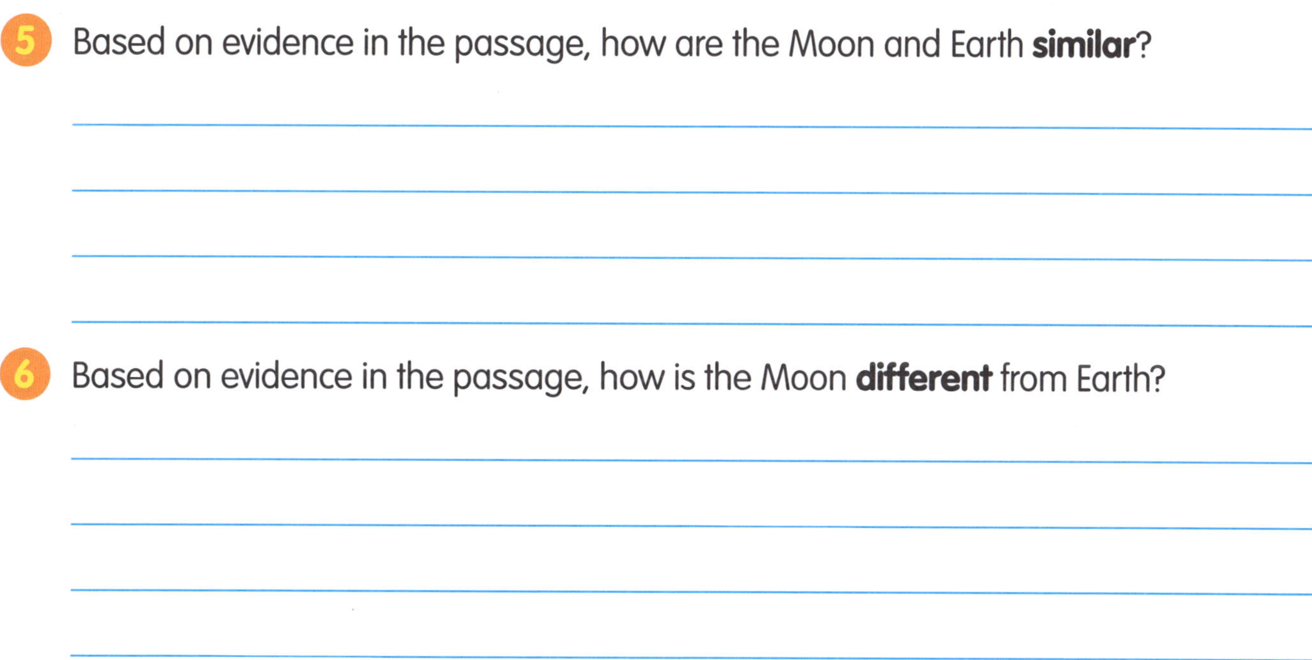

5 Based on evidence in the passage, how are the Moon and Earth **similar**?

6 Based on evidence in the passage, how is the Moon **different** from Earth?

LESSON 197

Conservation

Cause and Effect

To find cause and effect, we ask why something happens and what the result is.

Read the passage.

Highlight what happens to the land when people do not use soil and water correctly.

Underline how trees and plants bind soil together.

Put a box around what happens when too much native vegetation is removed.

Circle two natural phenomena that cause soil to erode.

Healthy, productive land can become dry and salty because of the way people use two natural resources: soil and water.

Trees and other plants bind soil together with their root systems. When too much native vegetation is removed — such as when land is cleared to graze animals — the structure of the soil breaks down. It dries out and erodes, either blown away by the wind or carried away by rain.

Soil can become compacted by overgrazing from cattle and other domesticated animals.

Circle the correct answers.

1 What **causes** healthy land to become dry and salty?

a too much native vegetation
b incorrect use of soil and water
c very strong winds
d too much rain

2 What **causes** soil to bind together?

a plants and trees
b air and water
c earthworms
d rock and clay

3 What **effect** does the removal of too much native vegetation have on soil? It causes it to …

a dry out.
b become damp.
c sprout weeds.
d bind together.

4 What **causes** soil erosion?

a heat and humidity
b very cold weather
c thunder and lightning
d wind and rain

5 How does overgrazing **affect** soil? It causes it to become …

a compacted.
b sandy.
c slimy.
d poisonous.

AC9E6LY05 Use comprehension strategies to connect content

Read the passage.

Highlight a positive effect of electricity and fuel on society.

Underline the negative effect that electricity and fuel have on the environment.

Circle the different sources of air pollution.

Industries make products and materials, such as electricity and fuel, which provide us with a modern, comfortable way of life — but they also pollute our natural resources.

The major sources of industrial air pollution are chemical plants, power stations, oil refineries and factories. However, cars pollute the air as much as industries do.

Under certain weather conditions, several air pollutants can have a combined effect that is worse than their individual effects. An example is photochemical smog, sometimes seen as a white haze over cities during summer. Photochemical smog forms on still days when sunlight drives chemical reactors between fuels and chemicals into the air. A product of these reactions is ozone, a gas harmful to people, animals and plants.

Colour the weather conditions necessary for photochemical smog to form.

Put a box around the gas that forms when fuels and chemicals interact in the presence of sunlight.

Highlight the effect of ozone on people, animals and plants.

6 Carefully explain the positive and negative **effects** of electricity and fuel on society and the environment.

7 List the major **causes** of air pollution.

8 Explain how ozone is formed.

LESSON 198

Working the Land

Finding the Main Idea and Supporting Details

To discover what a text is about, you need to look for the main idea or key point. Facts and details in the text can help you find the main idea.

Read the passage.

Circle the word that means *without a pause*.

Highlight three things crops require on a regular basis.

Put a box around the reason crops need fertilising.

Even when it's not the planting or harvesting seasons, crops still need constant attention, like watering, fertilising and pruning. Some crops require more care than others. The time needed for each crop will also depend on the weather, time of year and how long the crop has been growing.

Crops need fertilising to encourage growth. Pruning controls unwanted growth so trees can bear the most fruit possible. Watering and fertilising also help crops grow to their best potential.

Farmers use fertilisers as a way of adding nutrients already present in the soil. Fertilisers can be a huge expense for farmers, so it is very important to apply it in the right amounts at the right time to maintain a profitable farm.

Colour the reason crops have to be pruned.

Underline the reasons fertilisers need to be applied in the right amounts at the right time.

Circle the correct answers.

1. What is the passage **mainly** about?
   - a when to water crops
   - b planting and harvesting crops
   - c crops that require extra care
   - d caring for crops

2. Which three **details support the main idea**?
   - a Caring for crops depends on the weather.
   - b Fertilisers can be a huge expense for farmers.
   - c Crops need constant attention.
   - d Crops need fertilising to encourage growth.
   - e The soil contains nutrients.
   - f Watering and fertilising help crops grow to their best potential.

AC9E6LY05 Use comprehension strategies such as connecting to build literal and inferred meaning

Read the passage.

Underline the amount of time it takes for a newly planted banana plant to start producing fruit.

Highlight when a banana bunch is ready for picking.

A banana plant produces fruit about 15–18 months after planting. A banana bunch is ready for picking when the fruit is still green but just starting to yellow.

Harvesting bananas is hard work — bunches of bananas often weigh more than 50 kg! During the harvest season, two cutters and a driver go around the plantation cutting down the fruit and stacking them on a trailer. When transporting bananas, we always use padding to protect the skins from bruising.

Back at the shed, we hang up the bunches of bananas. Technology today makes this process a whole lot easier. We use a hydraulic lift, whereas a few years ago we had to carry the bunches on our backs!

Put a box around the clue that suggests that banana bunches are heavy.

Circle the reason farmers use padding when transporting bananas.

Colour why hanging up the bunches is easier today.

3 What is the passage **mainly** about?

4 Quote **details** from the passage that **support the main idea**.

Advertisements

Identifying Audience and Purpose

To identify the author's purpose in writing a text, it helps to work out who the text was written for. The language the author uses will show what his or her purpose is—to inform, persuade, instruct, or entertain.

Study the advertisement.

Underline why Fido does not remember going to the beach.

Highlight the rhetorical questions.

Circle how often the advertiser believes people should enjoy the outdoors.

Colour the benefits of an active lifestyle.

Highlight the Let's Get Moving campaign's slogan.

Put a box around where people can find out more about the Let's Get Moving campaign.

Do you remember when you last took Fido to the beach?

Do you remember how you played Frisbee and chased the waves in and out? Do you remember the smell of the clean, salty air and the feeling of sunshine on your face?

Fido doesn't remember.

Fido doesn't remember because it was such a long time ago. The thing about enjoying the outdoors is that it's best to do it regularly. An active lifestyle leads to increased fitness, better health and the prevention of illness. So why don't you plan for a healthier, happier lifestyle, starting this weekend. If you won't do it for Fido, at least do it for yourself.

Let's Get Moving!

Get out. Get active. Get alive.

A message brought to you by Let's Get Moving, a campaign to promote a healthy, active lifestyle. Find out more from www.letsgetmoving.gov.au

Circle the correct answers.

1. Who is this advertisement **aimed** at?
   - a people who own dogs
   - b people who do not exercise enough
   - c people who love animals
   - d people who exercise regularly
2. What is the main **purpose** of the advertisement? The main purpose of the advertisement is to encourage people to …
   - a get a dog.
   - b take their dogs to the beach.
   - c go to the beach more often.
   - d become more active.
3. What is the **purpose** of the rhetorical questions at the beginning of the text? They are designed to make the reader feel …
   - a enthusiastic.
   - b guilty.
   - c angry.
   - d afraid.

AC9E6LY03 Analyse how text structures and language features work together to meet the purpose of a text

Study the advertisement.

Highlight the sentence that refers to the child.

Underline the sentences that suggest that everyone in the car should wear a seatbelt.

Colour the sentence that suggests that people are likely to drive fast on country roads.

There are plenty of good reasons for wearing a seatbelt.

Shhhh.
This one is asleep.

If I don't wear a seatbelt I am only hurting myself.
Try telling that to your family.

Short trips are safe.
You can have a serious accident on any road, at any time.

Being in the backseat is safer than the front.
Serious injuries occur for passengers not wearing seatbelts.

I'm a good driver.
You might be, but what about the driver coming towards you?

Country roads are quiet.
Almost half of accidents on country roads involve speeding—that doesn't sound quiet or safe.

Police don't check if you're wearing seatbelts.
Yes, they do and penalties start at $250 for not wearing one.

A safety message from your local roads authority.

SEATBELTS SAVE LIVES.
SIMPLE.

Underline what happens if drivers are caught not wearing a seatbelt.

Circle the organisation responsible for the advertisement.

Put a **box** around the advertiser's slogan.

4 Who is the **target audience** for this advertisement?

5 The reasons for wearing a seatbelt are presented as a conversation between two people. Do you think this is an effective way of getting the message across? Give reasons for your answer.

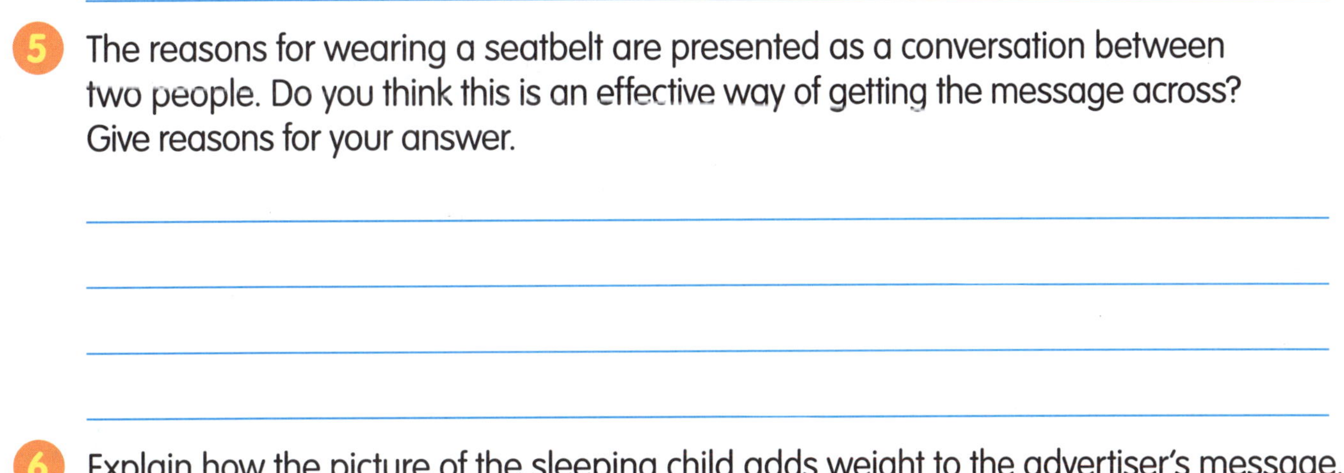

6 Explain how the picture of the sleeping child adds weight to the advertiser's message.

LESSON 200

The Universe

Reading Diagrams

Diagrams and pictures are often used to explain scientific or technical ideas. They help us understand the text by representing information in a visual form.

Study the diagram.

Put a box around the word that means *group*.

Highlight the word that means *turning*.

Circle the word that describes the shape of the galaxy.

Colour the name of a neutron star.

Circle the correct answers.

1. What is a rotating neutron star called?

   a a spiral b a cluster c a pulsar d a planet

2. Based on information in the pictures, which statement about planets is correct?

   a Planets are all the same size.
   b Planets are different sizes.
   c Planets shine brightly.
   d Planets have a spiral shape.

3. What is a cluster of stars?

   a a group of stars b a pair of stars c a single star d a very bright star

4. What does the picture suggest about galaxies?

   a A galaxy is a type of star.
   b There is only one galaxy in the universe.
   c Galaxies are smaller than stars.
   d Galaxies contain many stars.

AC9E6LA07 Identify and explain how images, figures, tables, diagrams, maps and graphs contribute to meaning

Study the diagram.

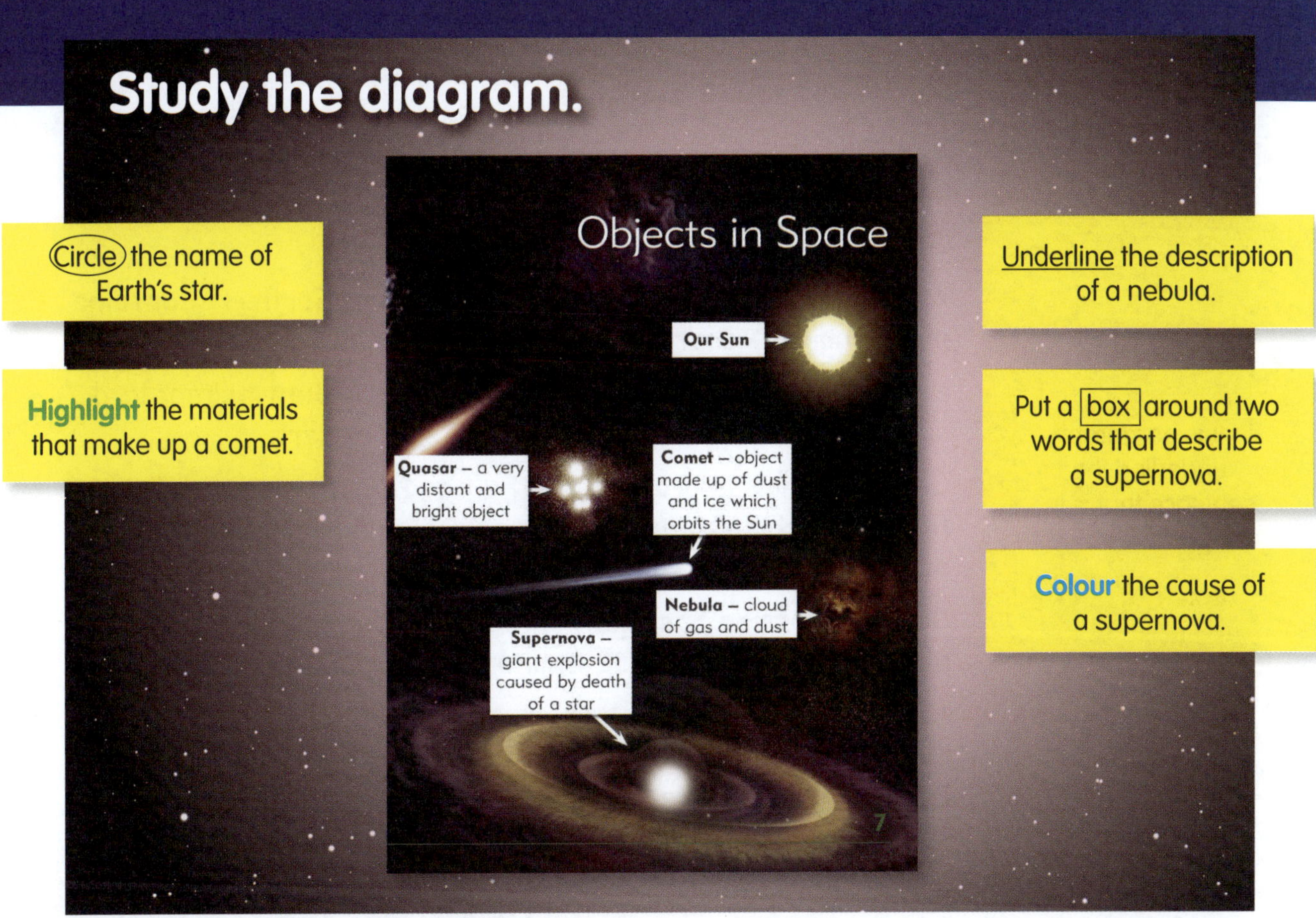

Circle the name of Earth's star.

Highlight the materials that make up a comet.

Underline the description of a nebula.

Put a box around two words that describe a supernova.

Colour the cause of a supernova.

Write a description of the following objects. Mention their shape, colour and anything else you notice about them.

5 a supernova ______________________________

____

____

____

6 a quasar ______________________________

____

____

____

7 a comet ______________________________

____

____

____

GRAMMAR LESSON 4

Active and Passive Voice

A sentence is in the **active voice** when the **subject** does the action. For example: **<u>The heart</u> (subject) <u>pumps</u> (action) blood around the body**. A sentence is in the **passive voice** when the action is done to the subject. For example: **<u>Blood</u> (subject) is pumped (action) around the body by the heart**.

Read the extract.

Africa

Africa is the second largest continent on Earth. It contains more than 50 countries.

North Africa is mostly dry and features Mount Kilimanjaro and the Sahara, the world's largest hot desert.

In this paragraph, underline the sentence that is in the **passive voice**.

Central Africa is crossed by the equator. The warm rain forests of this region are home to many rare animals such as forest elephants and leopards.

Southern Africa has many mines. They provide a major portion of the world's 12 main mineral resources.

In this paragraph, highlight the sentence that is in the **passive voice**.

Africa has the second highest population in the world, including hundreds of different ethnic groups. More than 2000 languages are spoken here.

Circle the correct answers.

In each sentence, identify the subject.

1 Many Africans speak English.

a Many b Africans c Many Africans d English

2 English is spoken by many Africans.

a English b many c Africans d many Africans

3 The Mediterranean Sea separates Africa from Europe.

a Mediterranean b The Mediterranean c The Mediterranean Sea

4 Africa is separated from Europe by the Mediterranean Sea.

a Europe b Africa
c Mediterranean d the Mediterranean Sea

5 Many African animals have been hunted to extinction.

a Many b African
c animals d Many African animals

AC9E6LA03 Explain how texts across the curriculum are typically organised into characteristic stages and phases depending on purposes, recognising how authors often adapt text structures and language features

6 **Identify the sentences that are in the passive voice.**

a ◯ African countries produce one third of the world's gold.

b ◯ One third of the world's gold is produced in African countries.

c ◯ Africa was colonised by European colonies in the late 1800s.

d ◯ European countries colonised Africa in the late 1800s.

e ◯ Snow covers the peak of Mount Kilimanjaro throughout the year.

f ◯ The peak of Mount Kilimanjaro is covered in snow throughout the year.

7 **Choose the correct verb to complete each sentence.**

a French _____ by the people of some African countries.

◯ spoken ◯ is spoken ◯ are spoken ◯ spoke

b In some African cultures, tribal clothing _____ during traditional ceremonies.

◯ are worn ◯ worn ◯ is wearing ◯ is worn

c Cocoa _____ by farmers in West Africa.

◯ is grown ◯ are grown ◯ grown ◯ were grown

d These artworks _____ by the people of West Africa.

◯ has created ◯ have created ◯ have been created ◯ has been created

e Nelson Mandela _____ president of South Africa in 1994.

◯ is elected ◯ will be elected ◯ had been elected ◯ was elected

8 **Complete each sentence in the passive voice.**

a The Zambian people made us feel welcome.

We were made to feel welcome ______________________________

b The African people gave the tourists directions.

The tourists were given directions ______________________________

c A group of volunteers is rebuilding the African village.

The African village is being rebuilt ______________________________

____

AC9E6LA03 Explain how texts across the curriculum are typically organised into characteristic stages and phases depending on purposes, recognising how authors often adapt text structures and language features

ASSESSMENT 2:

Antarctic Explorers

Lexile: 1060L

Roald Amundsen

Amundsen, the Norwegian explorer, was the first person to reach the South Pole. He originally planned to be the first person to reach the North Pole, but he changed his plans when Robert Peary arrived there first. Amundsen had a team of five men, all of whom were excellent skiers and experienced sled dog handlers. The team used 52 dogs to pull their four ice sleds across the snow. They arrived at the South Pole on 14 December 1911, and all returned home in good health.

Captain Robert Falcon Scott

Scott, the British explorer, had hoped to be the first person to reach the South Pole. Instead, he arrived there on 12 January 1912, one month after Amundsen. His team of four men travelled to the Pole on skis and on foot, hauling their own sleds. On the tragic return journey, the men faced frostbite, scurvy and a shortage of food. All five men died before they reached their base camp.

Sir Douglas Mawson

In 1912, Douglas Mawson, the Australian explorer and scientist, led a team of two other men, Ninnis and Mertz, to explore the far eastern region around Commonwealth Bay. Disaster struck when Ninnis fell down a crevasse and died. The supply sled and many of the dogs went down with him. Mertz later died of exposure, but miraculously Mawson, weak and exhausted, stumbled into camp weeks later. He had travelled 500 kilometres alone.

Lieutenant Ernest Shackleton

Shackleton, the British explorer, planned to cross the Antarctic continent in 1914, but his ship, the Endurance, was trapped by ice for many months. When the ice crushed the ship, the crew had to leave. They sailed to Elephant Island in the lifeboats, surviving on a diet of seal meat. Unfortunately, Elephant Island was deserted, so Shackleton and some of his crew sailed to South Georgia for help. The crew was eventually rescued.

Circle the correct answer for each question.

1 Who was the first person to reach the South Pole? **LITERAL**

- a Robert Peary
- b Robert Scott
- c Roald Amundsen
- d Douglas Mawson

2 How did Amundsen make sure his men would not become exhausted? **INFERENTIAL**

a He let his men have lots of breaks.
b He used dogs to pull the sleds.
c His men crossed the snow on skis.
d He gave his men nourishing food.

3 Which exploration team suffered the highest number of casualties? **LITERAL**

a Ernest Shackleton's
b Douglas Mawson's
c Roald Amundsen's
d Robert Scott's

4 When did the explorations described in the text take place? **LITERAL**

a in the 2nd decade of the 19th century
b in the 2nd decade of the 20th century
c in the 1st decade of the 19th century
d in the 1st decade of the 20th century

5 How would Scott have felt when he saw that Amundsen had reached the South Pole before him? **CRITICAL**

a pleased for Amundsen
b disbelieving
c extremely disappointed
d shocked

6 Which is the best inference? Elephant Island and South Georgia are … **INFERENTIAL**

a off the coast of Antarctica.
b part of South America.
c off the coast of Africa.
d in the Indian Ocean.

7 What type of text is this? **CRITICAL**

a a legend
b a historical recount
c a narrative
d a personal recount

8 What is the main purpose of this text? **CRITICAL**

a to issue a warning
b to tell a story
c to argue a point
d to give information

9 What conclusions can you draw about the conditions the explorers faced? **INFERENTIAL**

____

____

10 Explain what it means to die of 'exposure'. **VOCABULARY**

____

____

LESSON 201

Eye of the Future

Making Predictions

We can predict what is going to happen in a text based on clues in the words and pictures and what we already know.

Read the passage.

Circle where the narrator works.

Underline a sentence that shows that working at Chicken Heaven has had a positive effect on the narrator.

Life goes on as usual, except that I have started working at Chicken Heaven. I am nervous about learning the codes for different meals on the cash register but I enjoy it. I am so motivated I even do my homework and make my bed without being nagged.

Finally it is Tuesday. My grandmother is due home today. I am stuck at school and the day drags. I have trouble concentrating. The second my last class finishes, I am out the door. I ride home at a speed that an Olympic cyclist would envy.

Highlight what the narrator is nervous about.

Colour the sentence that suggests the reason the narrator is anxious to get home.

Fried Chicken

Circle the correct answers.

1 Which three events are most likely to happen?

- a The narrator will continue working at Chicken Heaven.
- b The narrator will never learn the codes for different meals on the cash register.
- c The narrator will learn the codes for the different meals on the cash register.
- d The narrator will visit her grandmother.
- e The narrator will become an Olympic cyclist.
- f The narrator will be in trouble for not concentrating in class.

2 What **evidence** is there in the text to support your **predictions**? Choose the two best options.

- a The narrator is nervous about learning the codes for different meals on the cash register.
- b The narrator enjoys working at Chicken Heaven.
- c The narrator can match the speed of an Olympic cyclist.
- d The narrator's grandmother is due back that day and she is anxious to get home.
- e The narrator goes straight home after her last class.
- f The narrator is stuck at school all day.

AC9E6LY05 Use comprehension strategies such as predicting to build literal and inferred meaning

Read the passage.

Circle two adjectives that describe the narrator's dreams.

Underline the sentence that suggests that the narrator is worried about having the Eye.

I nod, unable to imagine my brother Troy with the Eye. A week ago I wouldn't have imagined myself with the Eye either. "Do you still have normal dreams too? I mean weird dreams that can't possibly come true?"

My grandmother smiles. "Yes, I still have those. They keep me on my toes."

I sip my hot chocolate. "Is there anything I can do about the Eye?"

My grandmother laughs. "You can't turn it off, if that's what you mean." She becomes serious. "You must learn to live with it. Don't try to fight it."

Put a box around how long the narrator has had the Eye.

Highlight the advice the grandmother gives the narrator.

3 What kind of dreams do you think the narrator will have in the future?

4 What **evidence** is there in the passage that helped you make your **prediction**?

LESSON 202

Saving Atlantis

Summarising

A summary is a shortened version of the original text. To summarise a text, you need to look for the points and details that contain the most important information.

Read the passage.

Circle two words that show that there were hardly any people around the harbour.

Highlight what the old Greek lady was doing.

Underline the question Mia asked the old lady.

The busy harbour was strangely deserted! None of the fishing boats were in port and the cafes were empty. The only person they could see was an old Greek lady outside one of the cafes. She was hanging squid on lines to dry in the sun.

"Hello," said Mia as they approached her. "My name's Mia and this is Flynn. Where is everyone?"

"They're all at the celebrations," she said, turning and offering them a seat. "I can't stand the crowds myself."

The old lady pointed out to sea. "Today is the day the fishermen take all the villagers out to sea. They give thanks to the god of the sea, Poseidon, for good fishing."

Colour the old lady's reply to Mia's question.

Underline the reason the old woman was not at the celebrations.

Highlight the reason the fishermen had taken the villagers out to sea.

Circle the correct answers.

1 Which sentence best **summarises** paragraph 1?

- a There were no fishing boats in the port.
- b An old lady was hanging squid on lines to dry in the sun.
- c An old Greek lady was standing outside one of the cafes.
- d The harbour was deserted except for an old Greek lady.

2 Which sentence best **sums up** what happens in paragraphs 3 and 4?

- a Mia introduced herself and Flynn to the old lady.
- b The old lady told Mia and Flynn that everyone else was at the celebrations.
- c The old lady stayed behind because she didn't like crowds.
- d Mia asked the old lady where everyone was.

AC9E6LY05 Use comprehension strategies such as summarising to build literal and inferred meaning

Read the passage.

Circle the name of the sea god.

Highlight the reason the sea god created Atlantis.

Put a box around two adjectives that describe Atlantis.

The old lady's eyes lit up as she leaned closer. "Legend has it that the mighty sea god, Poseidon, made Atlantis for a woman he loved. Atlantis was a rich and beautiful place with silver topped temples, grand palaces, winding canals, magnificent harbours and lots of exotic animals."

"So what happened?" urged Flynn.

"Well, it seems the Atlanteans, who had everything they could wish for, became greedy and corrupt. Zeus, the king of all the gods, was so angry with them he banished the island to the bottom of the sea."

Circle the name of the king of all the gods.

Underline the reason the king of the gods became angry with the Atlanteans.

Colour what happened to Atlantis.

3 Write a **summary** of the passage. In your summary, include information about why Atlantis was created, what it looked like and what happened to it. Use the clues in the boxes to help you.

LESSON 203

Pardoning the National Turkey

Finding Facts and Information

To find facts and information in a text, we usually ask the questions **Who? What? Where?** or **When?** The answers can be clearly seen in the text.

Read the passage.

Circle the date on which the speech took place.

Put a box around the time the President started his speech.

Underline the official residence of the President of the United States of America.

Remarks by the President of the United States of America on Pardoning of the National Turkey

******

11:41 am 25 November 2009

North Portico, The White House, Washington D.C.

******

Happy Thanksgiving, everybody. Welcome to the White House. On behalf of Sasha and Malia and myself, we're thrilled to see you. I want to thank Walter Pelletier, chairman of the National Turkey Federation, and Joel Brandenberger, its president, for donating this year's turkey.

Highlight the names of the President's daughters.

Underline the people the President thanked.

Colour who Walter Pelletier was.

Circle the correct answers.

1. At what time of day did the President make this speech?
   - a in the afternoon
   - b at night
   - c in the morning
   - d at midday
2. Where was the President standing when he made the speech?
   - a on the North Portico of the White House
   - b in the Oval Office at the White House
   - c on the lawn outside the White House
   - d in the backyard of the White House
3. Where is the White House?
   - a in Texas
   - b in Washington D.C.
   - c in New York
   - d in North Carolina
4. Who did the President thank for donating the turkey?
   - a Walter Pelletier
   - b Joel Brandenberger
   - c Sasha and Malia
   - d Walter Pelletier and Joel Brandenberger

AC9E6LY05 Use comprehension strategies such as questioning to build literal meaning

Read the passage.

Circle the place the turkey would be sent to.

Put a box around how the President feels about the responsibility the American people have placed in him.

You know, there are certain days that remind me of why I ran for this office. And then there are moments like this — (laughter) — where I pardon a turkey and send it to Disneyland. (Laughter) But every single day, I am thankful for the extraordinary responsibility that the American people have placed in me. I am humbled by the privilege that it is to serve them and the tremendous honour it is to serve as Commander-in Chief of the finest military in the world — and I want to wish a Happy Thanksgiving to every service member at home or in harm's way. We're proud of you and we are thinking of you and we're praying for you.

Underline the President's role in the military.

Colour who the President is extending good wishes to.

5. Where was the President going to send the turkey?

6. What was the President thankful for?

7. What made the President feel humble?

8. What is the President's role in the military?

I Am Jack

Cause and Effect

To find cause and effect, we ask why something happens and what the result is.

Read the passage.

Highlight what Nanna needs help with.

Underline what happened when Nanna fell the previous year.

Circle the reason Nanna is unable to hear what Jack says about her.

Mum: Jack, Nanna needs help down the stairs.

Jack: That's my job. Three flights.

LFX Stairs.

Jack: Come on, Nan, give us your arm. She had a bad fall last year and broke her arm. Oh, don't worry, she can't hear; she's deaf.

He becomes Nanna struggling to go down the stairs.

Nanna: Have you got me, Jack? Oh, it's been a lovely afternoon. Do you like my new teeth? I've just had them renovated. I've eaten too many cookies. Hope they don't repeat. I won't be needing m'tea. Oh dear ... these stairs. I swear if I trip, I'll roll all the way down to the bottom.

Nanna wobbles. He transforms back to Jack.

Jack: Are you alright, Nan?

Colour the reason Jack pretends Nanna won't be needing any dinner.

Underline what Jack pretends might happen to Nanna if she trips.

Put a box around the word that is similar in meaning to *changes*.

Circle the correct answers.

1. What is the most likely **reason** Nanna needs help down the stairs?
   - a She has a broken arm.
   - b She is old and unsteady on her feet.
   - c She is deaf.
   - d She is scared of heights.
2. What **happened** when Nanna fell the previous year? Nanna broke her ...
   - a leg.
   - b hip.
   - c wrist.
   - d arm.
3. When Jack pretends to be Nanna, he says: "I've eaten too many cookies." According to Jack, how will this **affect** Nanna? Choose two options.
   - a The cookies have spoiled her appetite, and she won't be able to eat dinner.
   - b She is worried she may roll down the stairs.
   - c The cookies have spoiled her newly-renovated teeth.
   - d She is concerned she may suffer from indigestion later.

Read the passage.

Circle what Mum is doing in the kitchen.

Highlight the reason Mum does jumping jacks.

Underline what happens to Mum's hair when she does jumping jacks.

Jack encounters Mum doing star jumps in the kitchen.

Mum hates her thighs and the tops of her arms, so she's always doing star jumps, even in the middle of making dinner. Her hair fluffs up when she jumps. It's pretty funny. It wasn't so funny when Mum did it in the school car park the other day. What if someone saw her?

Mum: What, darling?

Jack: Don't call me that.

Mum: But you are my darling.

Jack: Mum, you promised, never again. I need to talk to you. Now.

Mum: When I've finished making dinner.

SFX Volcano begins.

That's a joke. Rob'll be here soon and then there'll be dinner, washing up, shower, homework. There'll be no time and I HAVE to talk to her. I think I'm in BIG trouble.

Put a box around a sentence that shows that Jack is annoyed with Mum.

Circle the word that indicates that Jack feels as if he is about to explode.

Colour why Jack wants to talk to Mum.

4 What **effect** does Mum hope doing star jumps will have?

5 What **causes** Mum's hair to fluff up?

6 What **causes** Jack to become annoyed?

LESSON 205

The Storytelling Stone

Visualisation

Visualising what we are reading about helps build better understanding of the text. Looking for key words in the text will help us create mental images.

Read the passage.

Circle where the Seneca boy hunted.

Underline where the boy was sitting when he heard the stone talk to him.

Put a box around the gift the boy gave the stone.

Highlight what the stone's stories were about.

Long ago, there was a Seneca boy who had been hunting in the forest all day. He sat on a stone to rest. As he sat, he heard a voice say, "Shall I tell you a story?"

The boy looked around to see who was talking to him. He could see no one. The voice spoke again. "Shall I tell you a story?" This time the boy realized that the voice was coming from the stone he was sitting on.

The boy wondered about the things the stone could tell. "Yes, I would like you to tell me a story," said the boy.

"First, you must give me one of the birds you caught today," said the stone.

The boy laid down one of his birds and the stone began. It told stories about strange creatures called stone giants, and flying heads that used to make war on the Seneca people.

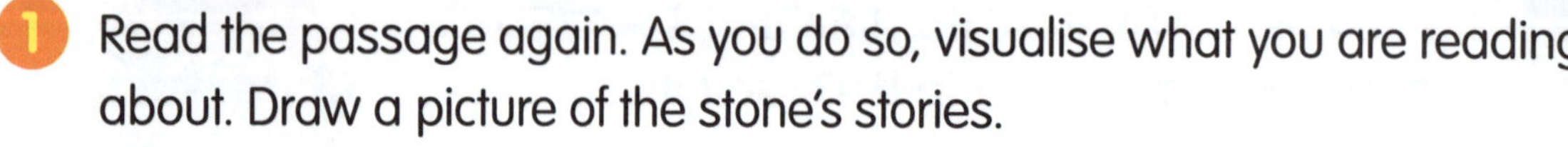

1. Read the passage again. As you do so, visualise what you are reading about. Draw a picture of the stone's stories.

AC9E6LY05 Use comprehension strategies such as visualising to build literal and inferred meaning

Read the passage.

Circle what the boy swapped for the stone's stories.

Underline who the boy brought to listen to the stone's stories.

As soon as the stone finished one story, it began another. The boy was spellbound.

Day after day for weeks, the boy returned, always swapping a bird for the stone's stories. He began to bring people from his village with him. Soon lots of people were coming to the stone to hear its stories. Then, one day the stone said to the boy, "I will no longer tell stories. Now it is your job to remember them and tell them to your people. Wherever you go to tell these legends, you will be welcomed and cared for.

The boy was given gifts in every Seneca village, just as he had given the stone a gift each day. He spread the stories among his people until he died. The stories are still told today.

Highlight what the stone said to the boy.

2 Read the passage again. As you do so, visualise what you are reading about. Draw a picture of people from the village listening to the stone's stories.

Multi-clause Sentences

A **clause** contains a **subject** and a **verb**. **Multi-clause** sentences contain two or more clauses. For example: **The children are playing indoors (clause 1) because it is raining (clause 2).** Counting the verbs will help you identify the number of clauses.

Read the extract.

The Sit-in

In this sentence, circle the **verbs**. → I felt a tug on my sleeve and turned around. It was Billy, who just smiled. I tried to smile back, but I was worried that we were all about to lose our jobs.

In this sentence, put a box around the **verbs**. → The workers chose three men who would speak on their behalf. For hours they negotiated with Mr Perkins, while the rest of us remained sitting.

In this sentence, highlight the **verbs**. → Finally, one of the workers returned and announced that four windows upstairs would stay open all day, and that the girls on my line could have two twenty-minute breaks during our twelve-hour shift.

With a show of hands, we voted to go back to work. No one saw much of Mr Perkins for the rest of the day.

In the final sentence, colour the **verbs**. → There was a rumour that he went home because he had lost his voice.

Circle the correct answers.

In each sentence, identify the number of clauses. Circle the verbs to help you.

1. It was Billy, who just smiled.
   a one b two c three d four

2. I tried to smile back, but I was worried about our jobs.
   a one b two c three d four

3. They negotiated with Mr Perkins, while the rest of us remained sitting.
   a one b two c three d four

4. No one saw much of Mr Perkins for the rest of the day.
   a one b two c three d four

5. My fellow workers had come downstairs and were demanding better working conditions, including fresh air while they stirred the large vats.
   a one b two c three d four

AC9E6LA05 Understand how embedded clauses can expand the variety of complex sentences to elaborate, extend and explain ideas

6 **Join the clauses to make sentences.**

	Main clause	Main Clause
a	Molly wanted to complain to Mr Perkins,	or her family would starve.
b	Molly had to work in the soap factory,	but he listened to their complaints.
c	Molly walked past Mr Perkins	and made her stay back for no pay.
d	Mr Perkins yelled at Molly	and joined the sit-in.
e	Mr Perkins was angry,	but she was afraid of losing her job.

7 **Now join these clauses to make sentences.**

	Main clause	Subordinate clause
a	Mr Perkins was angry	that produced soap.
b	Molly worked in a factory	if they didn't get back to work.
c	Molly was upset	because Molly was late.
d	Molly saw a woman	when Mr Perkins yelled at her.
e	Mr Perkins threatened to sack everyone	who was handing out pamphlets.

8 **Complete each sentence by adding another clause.**

a Molly couldn't afford to lose her job because her little brother was sick and

____

b When she got to the factory, Molly tried to explain why she was late, but

____

____

c Someone who was yelling even louder than Mr Perkins barged past a woman handing out pamphlets and ______________________________

____

d Molly rushed to help the woman, who assured her that ____________________

____

LESSON 206

Exploring Space

Making Inferences

To make inferences while reading, we have to use clues in the text. The clues help us find the answers that are hiding in the text.

Read the passage.

Highlight the reason some people are in favour of space exploration.

Underline the reasons some people are not in favour of space exploration.

Space stations allow people to live in space for long periods of time. Supporters believe that space exploration benefits people on Earth. Other people are worried about the cost of a space station and whether the discoveries are worthwhile.

The International Space Station (ISS) is the biggest structure ever built in space. Due to its size, people can live and work on the ISS for much longer than ever before. This allows scientists to gather information about the effects of living in space for long periods. This information could be helpful in working through the challenges of travelling to Mars.

Circle the word that means *global* or *worldwide*.

Colour the type of information scientists are able to gather on the International Space Station.

Circle the correct answers.

1. What can we **infer** about the people who live and work on the ISS? They come from …
   - a the United States.
   - b Russia and the United States.
   - c many different countries.
   - d China and the United States.
2. Which word is the **clue** to question 1's answer?
   - a scientists
   - b International
   - c Earth
   - d Mars
3. Based on **evidence** in the passage, which is the best **inference**?
   - a Not everyone agrees that the work done on space stations will benefit humanity.
   - b Everyone agrees that the work done on space stations will benefit humanity.
   - c Very few people think that the work done on space stations is worthwhile.
   - d Most people think that the work done on space stations is worthwhile.
4. Which words or phrases are the **clues** to question 3's answer?
   - a Space stations … Supporters
   - b Supporters … scientists
   - c benefits … worried
   - d Supporters … Other people

AC9E6LY05 Use comprehension strategies such as summarising to build inferred meaning

Read the passage.

Circle how distance is measured in space.

Highlight the speed at which light travels.

Underline the distance between Alpha Centauri and Earth.

Put a box around how long it takes light from Alpha Centauri to reach Earth.

Distances in space are measured in light years. This is the distance that light travels in one year.

A ray of light travels about 9.5 trillion kilometres in one year, or 9.5 million million kilometres—9 500 000 000 000 km. Scientists use light years to measure distances in the universe. They use light years to measure distances between galaxies and between stars.

Light years also tell how long the light has taken to reach Earth. Alpha Centauri is one of the closest stars to Earth. It is 4.3 light years from Earth. This means that the light from this star has taken 4.3 years to reach Earth. We see the star as it was 4.3 years ago.

5. What **inference** can we make about the speed at which light travels? Support your answer with a quote from the passage.

____

____

____

____

____

____

6. What **inference** can we make about distances in space? Support your answer with a quote from the passage.

____

____

____

____

____

LESSON 207

Discovering the Tomb of Tutankhamun

Word Study

Many English words come from Greek or Latin. Knowing common Greek and Latin affixes and word roots can help us work out the meaning of a word.

Read the passage.

Circle the word that describes the staircase.

Highlight the verb that is similar in meaning to were *obtained*.

Darkness and the iron testing rod told us that there was empty space. Perhaps another descending staircase, in accordance to the ordinary royal Theban tomb plan? Or maybe a chamber? Candles were procured — the all important tell-tale for foul gases when opening an ancient subterranean excavation — I widened the breach and by means of the candle looked in, while Lord Carnarvon, Lady E., and Callender with the Reises waited in anxious expectation.

Put a box around the word that shows that the excavation was under the ground.

Colour the noun that is formed from the verb *excavate*.

1. Find the words in the text that have the following Latin origins:
   - a *de-* (down) and *scandere* (to climb) __________
   - b *pro-* (for) and *curare* (to take care of) __________
   - c *sub-* (below) and *terra* (earth) __________
   - d *ex-* (out) and *cavus* (hollow) __________

2. Write a detailed definition for each of the words. Use context clues and the word's Latin origins to help you.
   - a __________
   - b __________
   - c __________
   - d __________

AC9E6LY09 Use knowledge of known words, word origins including some Latin and Greek roots, base words, prefixes, suffixes, letter patterns and spelling generalisations to spell new words including technical words

Read the passage.

Circle the noun that is formed from the base word *sense*.

Highlight the word that is similar in meaning to *statues* or *models*.

Our sensations and astonishment are difficult to describe, as the better light revealed to us the marvellous collection of treasures: two strange ebony-black effigies of a King, gold sandalled, bearing staff and mace, loomed out from the cloak of darkness; gilded couches in strange forms, lion-headed, Hathor-headed and beast infernal; exquisitely painted, inlaid and ornamental caskets; flowers; strange black shrines with a gilded monster snake appearing from within; quite ordinary-looking, white chests; finely carved chairs; a golden, inlaid throne; a heap of large, curious, white oviform boxes; beneath our very eyes, on the threshold, a lovely lotiform wishing-cup in translucent alabaster.

Underline the word that describes the shape of the white boxes.

Put a box around the word that describes the alabaster.

3 Find the words in the text that have the following Latin origins:

a *sensus* (feeling) ________________

b *ex-* (out) and *fingere* (to shape) ________________

c *ovus* (egg) and *forma* (shape) ________________

d *trans-* (through) and *lucere* (to shine) ________________

4 Write a detailed definition for each of the words. Use context clues and the word's Latin origins to help you.

a ________________

b ________________

c ________________

d ________________

LESSON 208

Trauma Alert

Sequencing Events

To identify the sequence of events in a text, we usually look at numbers and words that give clues to the order in which things happen.

Read the passage.

Highlight the message the emergency nurse receives.

Circle who accompanies the emergency nurse to the helipad.

Underline the description of the patient.

Colour the paramedic's report.

Put a box around where the patient is taken inside the ER.

Underline how the trauma team starts treating the patient.

A call comes in on my pager — MAJOR TRAUMA — HELIPAD. ARRIVAL 2 MINUTES.

Along with an Emergency Room (ER) doctor, I rush to the helipad. The helicopter doors open and the patient, a 19-year-old male lying on a stretcher, is rushed into the hospital.

On the way down to the ER, the paramedic begins his report, "... high-speed car accident ... unconscious at the scene ... tachycardic ... extensive blood loss ..."

Once inside the ER, we transfer the patient to a resuscitation bay (resus bay) and we are joined by the rest of the trauma team and an anaesthetist. We try to stabilise the patient as our team's assessment begins.

1 Number the following events in the order in which they happened.

- [ ] The patient is taken to the resuscitation bay.
- [ ] The emergency nurse hurries to the helipad.
- [ ] The trauma team begins its assessment of the patient.
- [ ] The emergency nurse receives a call advising him of a patient's arrival.
- [ ] The paramedic reports on the patient's condition.
- [ ] The rest of the trauma team and an anaesthetist join the ER doctor and nurse.
- [ ] The emergency nurse sees a young male lying on a stretcher.
- [ ] Medical staff prepare to move the patient into the hospital.
- [ ] The trauma team attempts to stabilise the patient.

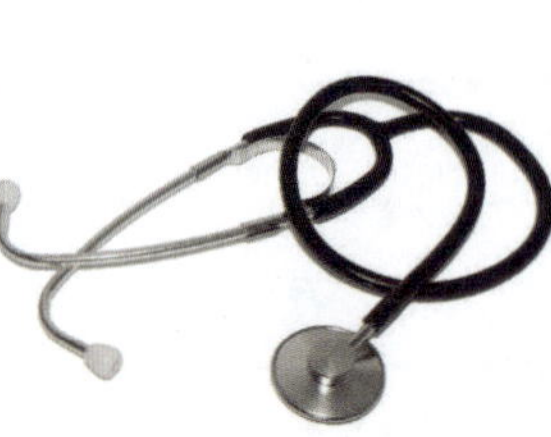

AC9E6LY05 Use comprehension strategies to build literal and inferred meaning

Read the passage.

Highlight the reason the patient is placed on a ventilator.

Put a box around the reason the patient is sedated.

Colour what happens once the tube has been put in place.

The patient cannot breathe properly, so we decide to put a breathing tube down his throat and into his lungs to allow a ventilator to breathe for him.

The doctor signals that it is time to administer the medications to sedate and paralyse the patient. This is so he feels no pain. The doctor puts the tube down the patient's throat and his chest starts to rise and fall more easily with the help of the ventilator. A chest X-ray is taken to make sure the tube is in the right place and inflating both lungs correctly.

The patient is now stable enough to transfer to radiology for further scans to check for possible neck and head injuries.

Underline how the doctor is able to tell if both lungs are inflating correctly.

Circle where the patient is taken for further scans.

Highlight the reason further scans are necessary.

2 Rewrite the following sentences so that they are in the correct order.

The patient needs further scans to check for possible injuries. Once he has been stabilised, he is moved to radiology. Inserting the tube down the patient's throat and into his lungs can be a painful experience, so first he must be sedated. The patient is having difficulty breathing and is placed on a ventilator. With the tube in, the patient can breathe more easily.

LESSON 209

Community Survey

Fact or Opinion?

A fact is a statement that can be proved to be true; for example: A spider has eight legs. An opinion is a statement that expresses a belief or feeling; for example: Spiders are ugly.

Read the passage.

Highlight the reason for the survey.

Underline who will take part in the survey.

In question 1, circle the instruction in parentheses.

Dear Resident,

The survey below is part of a project to help understand and build the local community. It is being given to each household in the Trevally district.

About living in Trevally

1 How long have you been at your current address in the Trevally district? (Please check a box.)

- ☐ Less than 12 months
- ☑ 1–2 years
- ☐ 5–10 years
- ☐ more than 10 years

2 How much do you agree with the following statements? (Please circle a number.)
1 = strongly disagree 7 = strongly agree

a) When I go shopping I am likely to meet friends and acquaintances.

1 2 (3) 4 5 6 7

b) It is safe to walk around the area at night.

1 2 3 4 5 6 (7)

Colour how long the person filling in the survey has lived in Trevally.

In question 2b, put a box around the words that show to what extent the resident agrees.

1 Are the following statements facts, or opinions? Write **F** next to the facts, and **O** next to the opinions.

a Every household in the Trevally district received a form to fill in. ________

b The purpose of the survey is to help build a better community. ________

2 In the following answers, is the resident stating a fact, or expressing an opinion? Write **F** next to the facts, and **O** next to the opinions.

a I have lived in my home for more than a year. ________

b I sometimes run into friends and acquaintances when I go shopping. ________

c I believe that Trevally is a very safe place to live in. ________

AC9E6LY05 Use comprehension strategies such as questioning to build literal and inferred meaning

Read the passage.

In question 4a, highlight the words that show to what extent the resident agrees.

Circle the deadline for placing the completed survey in the mail.

Please complete the survey and put it in the mail by Friday, 31 August in the reply paid envelope provided.

Your life experience

4 How much do you agree with the following statements? (Please circle a number.)
1 = disagree strongly   7 = agree strongly

a) I am happy about my housing situation.
1 2 3 4 5 6 (7)

b) In general, I have excellent health.
1 2 3 4 (5) 6 7

c) I often feel rushed, pressured and too busy.
(1) 2 3 4 5 6 7

In question 4b, put a box around what the survey is asking.

In question 4c, colour the words that show to what extent the resident agrees.

3 Quote two **facts** about how the survey is to be returned to the Mayor of Trevally.

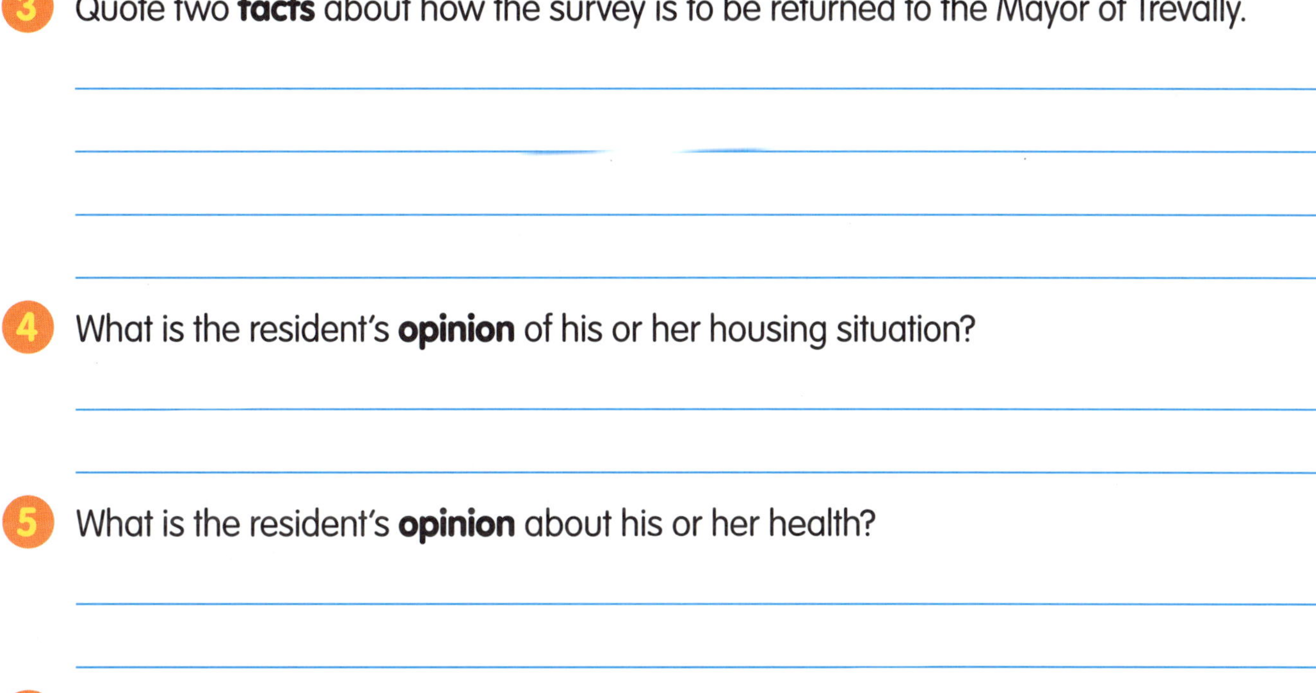

4 What is the resident's **opinion** of his or her housing situation?

5 What is the resident's **opinion** about his or her health?

6 What is the resident's **opinion** about feeling rushed, pressured or too busy?

LESSON 210

Water

Cause and Effect

To find cause and effect, we ask why something happens and what the result is.

Read the passage

Highlight what happens to chemical fertilisers and pesticides when it rains.

Circle what can happen to algae when chemicals enter the water.

Underline how algal bloom affects the water.

Put a box around what fish and plants need to live.

Colour how acid rain is formed.

Farmers use chemical fertilisers and pesticides on their crops. When it rains, some of these chemicals may wash into rivers. This can cause algal bloom in lakes and rivers. Algal bloom is the rapid growth of algae on the water's surface. It blocks out sunlight and uses up oxygen in the water. Fish and plants need oxygen to live, so algal bloom can kill them. Some algae are poisonous and make the water undrinkable.

When heavily polluted air mixes with the water in clouds, it falls back to earth as acid rain. Acid rain can make the soil so acidic that trees can't grow.

Circle the correct answers.

1. Which of the following can **cause** algal bloom in lakes and rivers?
   - a rain
   - b chemicals
   - c certain types of fish
   - d cloudy weather

2. What can **happen** when farmers use chemical fertilisers and pesticides on their crops? The chemicals can ...
   - a make the soil more fertile.
   - b kill the crops.
   - c evaporate and poison the air.
   - d get washed into rivers.

3. What can **cause** fish and water plants to die? Lack of ...
   - a oxygen
   - b carbon dioxide
   - c rain
   - d chemicals

4. What **causes** acid rain? Polluted air mixing with water ...
   - a in rivers and lakes
   - b in the atmosphere
   - c underground
   - d in the ocean

5. How does acid rain **affect** the environment?
   - a It encourages weeds to grow.
   - b It prevents trees from growing.
   - c It causes heavier than usual rainfall.
   - d It causes droughts.

AC9E6LY05 Use comprehension strategies to connect content

Read the passage.

Highlight the reason wetlands are able to hold large amounts of water.

Underline the reason wetlands were once used as dumping grounds for trash and sewage.

Colour the reason many wetlands were destroyed.

Wetlands act as natural water filters. They are like sponges, with the soil holding large amounts of water. When there is heavy rain, wetlands absorb the water and then release it slowly later. This helps prevent flooding of surrounding land.

Wetlands were once seen as damp, dangerous places that caused diseases. They were used as dumping grounds for trash and sewage, and many wetlands were destroyed to create more land for agriculture and building.

Heavy rain then went straight into rivers, rather than wetlands, and contributed to flooding. Because wetlands are breeding grounds for fish and other aquatic life, the loss of wetlands damaged fishing industries.

Underline how the destruction of wetlands affected the environment.

Highlight why the destruction of wetlands damaged fishing industries.

6. **Why** did people use wetlands as dumping grounds for trash and sewage?

7. **Why** were many wetlands destroyed?

8. Carefully explain how the destruction of wetlands **affected** industry and the environment.

Adjectival Clauses

Adjectival clauses give information about nouns or pronouns. They are introduced by the relative pronouns **who, whose, which** or **that** and the relative adverbs **where, when** and **why**. For example: **We spoke to the scientists <u>who work for the Department of the Environment</u>** (adjectival clause).

Read the extract.

In this sentence, circle the **relative pronoun** and highlight the **adjectival clause**.

In this sentence, put a box around the **relative pronoun** and colour the **adjectival clause**.

In this sentence, circle the **relative pronouns** and underline the **adjectival clauses**.

Emma Watson

Emma Charlotte Duerre Watson was born in Paris and brought up in Oxfordshire. She landed the role of Hermione Granger in the *Harry Potter* films when she was just nine years old. She spent the next ten years, during which she completed primary and high school, acting in eight *Harry Potter* films.

Watson uses her position as a United Nations Goodwill Ambassador to promote the UN's HeForShe campaign, which asks men and boys to speak out against gender inequality.

Supporters make the following statement and commitment when they sign up: "I am one of billions of men who believe equality for women is a basic human right that benefits us all. And I commit to taking action against gender discrimination and violence in order to build a more just and equal world."

Circle the correct answers.

In each sentence, identify the missing word.

1 Feminism is the belief _____ men and women should be treated equally.
a which b who c whose d that

2 That was the year _____ casting began for the first *Harry Potter* film.
a where b which c when d why

3 Emma Watson was born in Paris, _____ is the capital of France.
a which b where c who d whose

4 Watson went to New York City, _____ she delivered a speech at the UN headquarters.
a where b who c which d that

5 Emma Watson, _____ has starred in many films, is best known for her role as Hermione Granger.
a whose b who c which d that

AC9E6LA05 Understand how embedded clauses can expand the variety of complex sentences to elaborate, extend and explain ideas

6 **Join the clauses to make sentences.**

	Main clause	Adjectival clause
a	J K Rowling is the author	where she met Harry and Ron.
b	Hermione attended Hogwarts,	that Emma Watson acts in.
c	Watson has been nominated for awards,	which are all bestsellers.
d	I told him about the movie	many of which she has won.
e	I have read the *Harry Potter* books,	who wrote the *Harry Potter* books.

7 **Complete each sentence with an adjectival clause from the box below.**

a The girl ______________________________
is a young Emma Watson.

b The *Harry Potter* movies, ______________________________,
have made millions of dollars at the box office.

c J K Rowling, ______________________________,
wrote the *Harry Potter* series.

who is a bestselling author **which are extremely popular**
whose photo is on the poster

8 **Join each pair of sentences with the word in brackets. You may need to change the word order.**

a Emma Watson visited Zambia. She promoted education for girls in Zambia. (where)

____

____

b The man is concerned about gender equality. He has joined HeForShe. (who)

____

____

c I belong to the organisation. The organisation promotes gender equality. (that)

____

____

ASSESSMENT 3:

The Snake-haired Monster

Lexile: 1050L

Zeus, the king of the Greek gods, fell in love with Danae, a beautiful mortal woman. They had a son called Perseus. A prophecy foretold that Perseus would one day kill his grandfather, so to protect himself, the grandfather placed Danae and Perseus in a wooden chest, which he cast into the sea. The chest eventually came ashore on the island of Seriphos, where mother and son were rescued by a kindly old couple.

The king of Seriphos fell in love with Danae, but she did not return his love. The king knew that Perseus would protect his mother, so to get the young man out of the way, he sent him to kill the Medusa, a monster with the face of a beautiful woman, but with writhing snakes for hair. Anyone who looked at her was instantly turned to stone.

The gods took pity on Perseus and, to help him in his quest, gave him a magic shield, polished like a mirror, and a powerful sword. They told him to look for the Graea, the old grey women, who would tell him how to find the Medusa.

Perseus set out in search of the Graea, but when he eventually found them, they refused to help him. The two wizened old women had only one eye and one tooth between them, and constantly bickered over whose turn it was to have them. While they were tussling for the eye, Perseus snatched it from them. "Tell me where she is," he threatened, "or you will not get this back."

The Graea relented, and told Perseus how to find the Medusa. Perseus returned their eye, but only after he had taken from them some items to help him on his mission: a cap of invisibility, the winged shoes of swiftness, and a satchel in which to place the Medusa's head.

After a long journey, Perseus finally found the Medusa. He knew that if he looked directly at her, he would be turned to stone, so he came up with a clever plan. Rather than looking directly at the Medusa, he looked at her reflection in his polished shield. He was then able to use the magic sword to cut off her head, which he placed in the satchel.

His task completed, Perseus prepared to return to Seriphos. Little did he know, however, that he would experience many more adventures before he saw the island again.

Circle the correct answer for each question.

1 Who was Perseus' father? **LITERAL**

a the king of Seriphos **b** Danae

c Zeus **d** Medusa

2 What did the grandfather most likely think would happen to the chest containing Danae and Perseus? He most likely thought the chest would … **CRITICAL**

a sink and its occupants would drown.
b float to a distant land.
c break up and its occupants saved.
d keep on floating forever.

3 How did the gods help Perseus? The gods gave Perseus … **LITERAL**

a a cap and shoes with special powers.
b a magic shield and sword.
c directions to the Medusa's cave.
d a magic tooth and eye.

4 Which sentence is true? Perseus … **INFERENTIAL**

a knew where to find the Medusa.
b could not find the Medusa.
c did not want to find the Medusa.
d needed help to find the Medusa.

5 Why was Perseus able to get the eye away from the Graea? While tussling over the eye, the Graea would have been … **INFERENTIAL**

a distracted.
b temporarily blind.
c temporarily deaf.
d unable to move.

6 Which is the odd word out? **VOCABULARY**

a bickered
b argued
c squabbled
d persuaded

7 Which words best describe Perseus? **CRITICAL**

a arrogant and reckless
b kind and generous
c clever and brave
d nervous and helpless

8 What type of text is this? **CRITICAL**

a a fable
b a myth
c a historical recount
d a personal recount

9 Use clues in the text to explain what a prophecy is. **VOCABULARY**

____

____

10 How did Perseus avoid being turned into stone? **LITERAL**

____

____

LESSON 211

Assignment Fiasco

Cause and Effect

To find cause and effect, we ask why something happens and what the result is.

Read the passage.

Highlight why Hannah went to sit under the tree.

Underline words that help us work out how Josh felt when Hannah said she was going to sit under the tree.

Circle the words that show how close Hannah was to the dead snake.

"Oh, I can't work with you," said Hannah. "This is insane. I need some air." She grabbed her books and looked out the window. "I'm going to sit under that tree."

"Wh...? Wha...? What tree?" stammered Josh. Hannah was already out the door and headed for his snake tree. All he could do was watch through the window as she walked down the stairs and sat right under the branch. He couldn't help but notice how undead the snake looked. Normally, he would have been pleased. Right now, he felt sick. Josh reckoned it would take Hannah about three seconds to notice the snake. He began to count.

"AAAAAAAAAHHHHHHHHHHHHHHHHHHHH!"

Colour how long Josh thought it would be before Hannah noticed the snake.

Put a box around Hannah's reaction when she saw the snake.

Circle the correct answers.

1. **Why** did Hannah go and sit under the tree?
   - a It was hot and stuffy in the library.
   - b She didn't want to work with Josh.
   - c She thought the fresh air would help her think.
   - d She was feeling sick.
2. What **effect** did Hannah's decision to sit under the tree have on Josh? He felt a sense of …
   - a excitement.
   - b disappointment.
   - c shock.
   - d pleasure.
3. What was the most likely **reason** there was a dead snake in the tree?
   - a A bird had dropped it there.
   - b A cat had dragged it there.
   - c The science class had left it there.
   - d Josh had put it there.
4. **Why** did Josh think it would take Hannah only three seconds to notice the snake? It was …
   - a a bright colour.
   - b right above Hannah's head.
   - c smelling badly.
   - d very big.
5. What **happened** when Hannah saw the snake? She …
   - a screamed.
   - b fainted.
   - c ran away.
   - d reached up to touch it.

AC9E6LY05 Use comprehension strategies to connect content

Read the passage.

Highlight the reason Josh sat behind Hannah.

Underline the reason Hannah was excited.

Colour why Hannah would still be sticking to the Assignment Quest rules if she used Emma's idea.

Hannah sat with Emma, a girl from the year above. Josh hid in the seat behind Hannah, waiting for another chance to talk to her. Then he overheard Hannah's plan.

"That is such a good idea," cried Hannah with excitement. "It gets me out of working with Super Pain and I'm not cheating or breaking any of the Assignment Quest rules."

"Exactly," agreed Emma. "You're still working in a team and you're not swapping him for someone else. You're just getting him to do what he's best at — which in this case isn't much."

They both giggled.

Josh heard Hannah say, "So what's the web address for this site, Emma? I'd better write it down."

Underline the words that suggest that Emma does not have a high opinion of Josh's abilities.

Circle where Hannah intends to find help with her assignment.

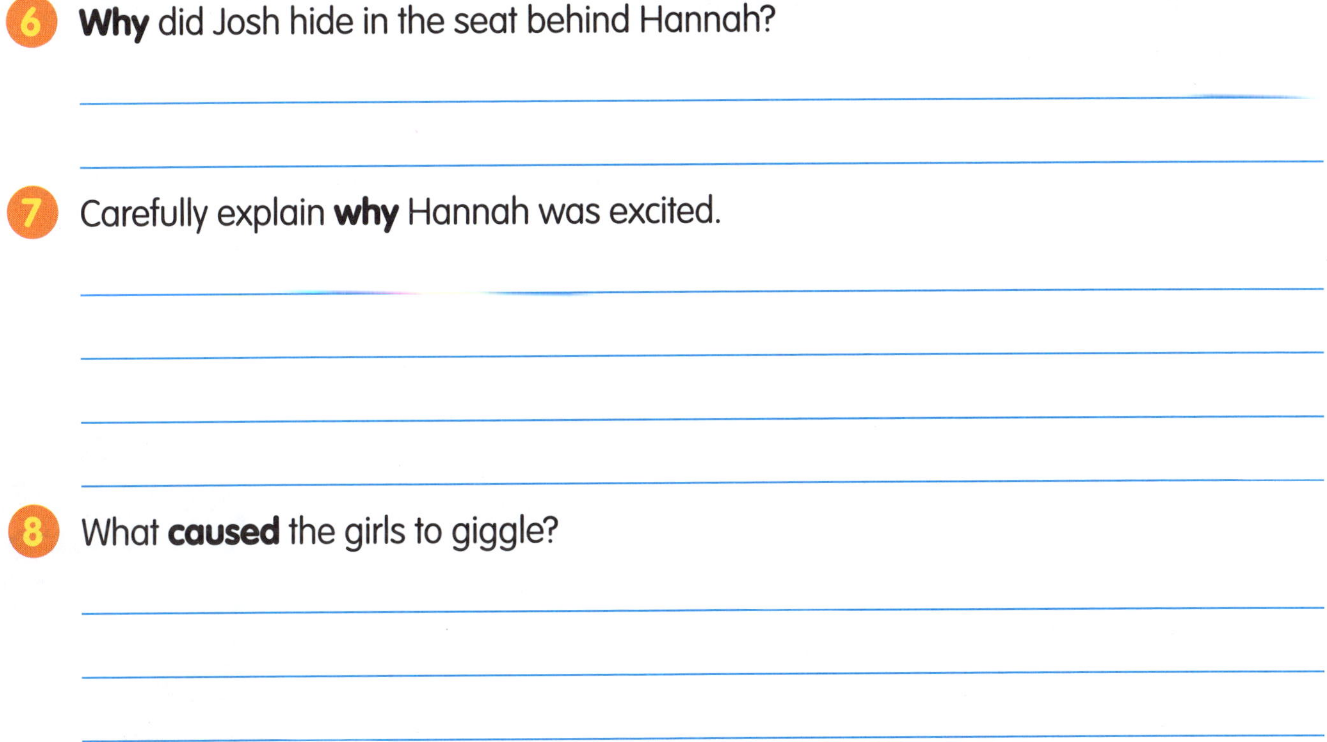

6 **Why** did Josh hide in the seat behind Hannah?

7 Carefully explain **why** Hannah was excited.

8 What **caused** the girls to giggle?

LESSON 212

The Complicator

Point of View

To identify the author or a character's point of view in a text, we need to look at his or her choice of words and details. These will help to reveal their beliefs, personal judgements or attitudes.

Read the passage.

Circle the word that shows how Rory felt about school.

Highlight the words that indicate that Mr Logie did not want to encourage Rory to interrupt the lesson.

Underline the words that show that Mr Logie felt he was taking a chance in allowing Rory to ask a question.

School was even more complicated than home. Rory enjoyed school. He knew the answers to most of the questions Mr Logie asked the class, but everyone was always in such a hurry.

"Today we are going to learn about coal," began Mr Logie warily, trying not to look in Rory's direction. But Rory's arm shot up and waved about. Mr Logie decided to risk it. "Yes, what is it, Rory?"

"Please, sir, will we be learning about black coal, brown coal or charcoal?"

"Coal!" thundered Mr Logie. 'JUST — ABOUT — COAL! And I am warning you, Rory! I happen to think that sending complicated-boys-who-ask-too-many-questions down coal mines is A VERY GOOD IDEA!"

Colour the question that Rory asked Mr Logie.

Put a box around the word that suggests that Mr Logie shouted at Rory.

Underline the words that best express Mr Logie's opinion of Rory.

Circle the correct answers.

1. How did Rory **feel** about school? He …
   - a hated it.
   - b liked it.
   - c thought it was simple.
   - d found it boring.
2. Which word is the **clue** to question 1's answer?
   - a hurry
   - b complicated
   - c knew
   - d enjoyed
3. How did Mr Logie **feel** about Rory? Mr Logie **thought** that Rory …
   - a was a nuisance.
   - b was conscientious.
   - c was clever.
   - d had good ideas.
4. What is the **clue** to question 3's answer? Mr Logie …
   - a asked Rory to answer the questions.
   - b liked to listen to Rory's ideas.
   - c said that Rory asked too many questions.
   - d thought that Rory knew a lot about coal.

AC9E6LY05 Use comprehension strategies such as questioning to build inferred meaning

Read the passage.

Circle the word that sums up the author's opinion of Parrot the dog.

Highlight the author's description of Parrot.

Put a box around Rory's reaction the first time he saw Parrot.

By this time, Lettice was ready to play with her ridiculous dog called Parrot.

Sorry to be rude about a small animal, but she was ridiculous. She looked like a parrot without feathers. She even had a crest like a parrot. Rory gawped the first time he saw Parrot and wondered what unpleasant disease she had.

"Chinese Crested!" said Lettice. "Very simple — no brushing, no fleas, no walking. And she makes a good hot water bottle."

"It looks very ... er, um, fragile," said Rory, trying to be polite.

Lettice giggled. "Hideous, you mean! But I love her."

Underline the words that show that there was something wrong with Parrot.

Circle the word that is similar in meaning to *delicate*.

Colour how Lettice feels about Parrot.

5 What is the author's **opinion** of Parrot the dog? Support your answer with quotes from the passage.

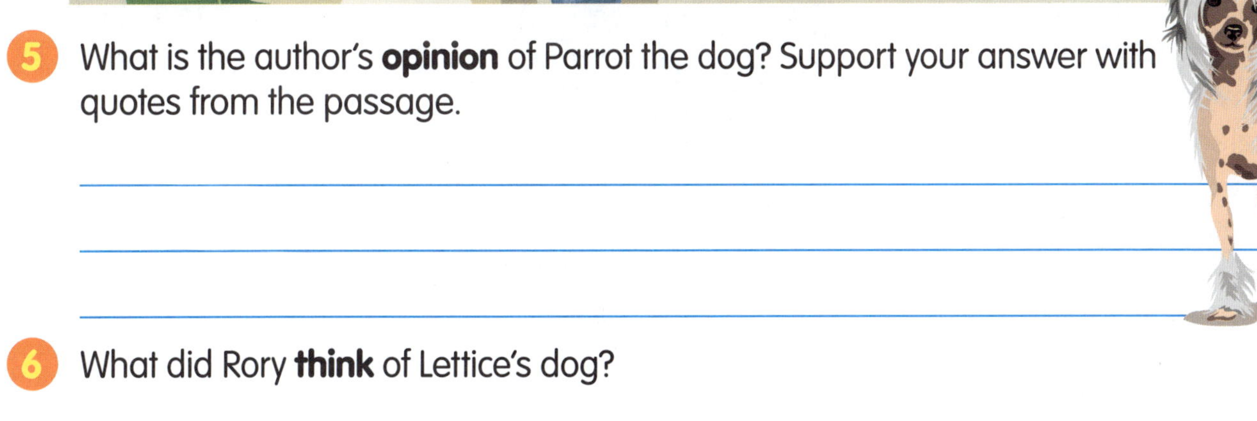

6 What did Rory **think** of Lettice's dog?

7 What is Lettice's **opinion** of her dog? Support your answer with quotes from the passage.

LESSON 213

Robin Hood

Making Connections

Linking a text to other texts you have read is a great way to build understanding. Look for key words and phrases in the texts to make the connections.

Read the passages.

Text 1

As they neared the Abbey, Robin walked in front of the rest and held his bow in his free hand. Presently he came to a stream and heard sounds of a jovial song floating towards him. He hid under a bush and watched alertly. At length, approaching the far bank, Robin espied a knight, clad in chain armour and very merry.

He sang, in a lusty voice, a hearty woodland song. "Now by my bones!" thought Robin, puzzled, "but I have heard this song before."

In both texts, circle where Robin sat and waited.

In both texts, **highlight** the sounds Robin heard.

In both texts, underline the description of the man on the opposite bank.

Text 2

Steadily Robin pressed forward till he came to a stream that dipped in and out among the willows and rushes on the banks.

As he sat down to rest and take his bearings, he heard snatches of a jovial song floating to him from the farther side.

Presently the willows on the other bank parted and there emerged a stout friar in a long cloak, tied with a cord in the middle. On his head was a knight's helmet and in his hand was a huge pasty pie.

Circle the correct answers.

1. What information appears in **both texts**? Robin came to …
   - a some bushes.
   - b some willow trees.
   - c a stream.
   - d some rushes.
2. What information appears in **both texts**? Robin heard someone singing …
   - a a woodland song.
   - b a happy song.
   - c a sad song.
   - d a folk song.
3. What information appears in **Text 1**? The man Robin saw was wearing …
   - a a knight's helmet.
   - b a long cloak.
   - c a leather cloak.
   - d chain armour.
4. What extra information does **Text 2** give us about the man Robin saw? He was …
   - a eating a pie.
   - b tying a cord around his middle.
   - c singing in a loud voice.
   - d holding his helmet in his hand.

AC9E6LY05 Use comprehension strategies to connect content

Text 1

Robin called out suddenly upon the knight, fitting an arrow as he did so.

"I pray you, Sir Knight, to carry me across this stream," said Robin.

"Put down your bow, forester," shouted the knight, "and I will safely carry you across the stream."

While Robin was searching his memory to fit a name to this courteous knight, the latter had waded across to him.

The knight carried Robin safely across the stream.

"Now, gossip, you shall carry me over this stream," said the knight serenely. "One good turn deserves another, as you know."

In both texts, **highlight** Robin's request to the man to carry him across the water.

In both texts, underline the man's answer to Robin's request.

In one of the texts, **colour** the words that show that Robin thinks he knows the man.

Put a box around the final paragraph in both texts.

Text 2

Robin seized his bow and fitted an arrow. "Hey, Friar!" he sang out, "carry me over the water."

"Put down your bow, fellow," the friar shouted back, "and I will bring you over the stream."

The friar waded across the stream and took Robin upon his back. He spoke neither good word nor bad till he came to the other side.

Robin leaped lightly off his back, and said, "I am much beholden to you good father."

"Beholden, say you!" rejoined the other, drawing his sword; "then you shall repay your score. In short, my son, you must carry me back again."

5 Write a paragraph that briefly describes what both texts tell us about the events.

6 List at least three ways in which the texts give a different interpretation of the events.

LESSON 214

The Lake Isle of Innisfree

Figurative Language

Alliteration repeats consonant sounds. **Onomatopoeia** imitates sounds. **Similes** compare one thing to something unlike itself by using the words *like* or *as*. **Metaphors** make a more direct comparison. They do not contain the words *like* or *as*. **Personification** is a type of metaphor that gives animals and objects human qualities.

Read the passage.

Circle the word that describes the glade.

Highlight the words that describe how the poet envisions peace coming to the Isle.

Put a box around the word that suggests that the morning is misty.

I will arise and go now, and go to Innisfree,
And a small cabin build there, of clay and wattles made:
Nine bean-rows will I have there, a hive for the honey-bee;
And live alone on the bee-loud glade.

And I shall have some peace there, for peace comes dropping slow,
Dropping from the veils of the morning to where the cricket sings;
There midnight's all a glimmer, and noon a purple glow,
And evening full of the linnet's wings.

Underline the sound that the poet imagines he will hear in the morning.

Colour the words that suggest that at night the poet will see lots of stars in the sky.

Circle the words that suggest that there will be lots of birds flying about in the evening.

Circle the correct answers.

1. What **image** of peace does the poet's description in lines 5 and 6 create? The poet creates an image of peace as something …
   - a hard to hold on to.
   - b soft and gentle.
   - c harsh and shrill.
2. Which of the following is a **metaphor**?
   - a Nine bean-rows
   - b bee-loud glade
   - c veils of the morning
   - d where the cricket sings
3. Which of the senses is the poet appealing to when he **compares** noon to a purple glow?
   - a sight
   - b hearing
   - c touch
   - d smell
4. Which two senses is the poet appealing to in the final line?
   - a sight
   - b hearing
   - c touch
   - d smell

AC9E6LA08 Identify authors' use of vivid, emotive vocabulary, such as metaphors, similes, personification, idioms, imagery and hyperbole

Read the passage.

Highlight three metaphors in stanza 1.

Underline an example of alliteration in stanza 2.

And I shall have some peace there, for peace comes dropping slow,
Dropping from the veils of the morning to where the cricket sings;
There midnight's all a glimmer, and noon a purple glow,
And evening full of the linnet's wings.

I will arise and go now, for always night and day
I hear lake water lapping with low sounds by the shore;
While I stand on the roadway, or on the pavements grey,
I hear it in the deep heart's core.

Circle the colours that compare the brightness of the Isle with the dullness of the city.

Colour the line that indicates that the poet hears the sounds of the lake no matter where he is.

5 Use ideas from the poem to help you complete the following **similes**.

a Peace descended on the Isle like ______________________

____

b The morning mist hung like ______________________

____

c The stars in the sky shone as ______________________

____

6 What **figure of speech** is *lake water lapping with low sounds*?

____

7 Why are the repeated *l* sounds in *lake water lapping with low sounds* an effective way of describing the sounds by the shore?

____

____

____

Daedalus and Icarus

Drawing Conclusions

To draw conclusions from a text, we have to use clues to make our own judgements. The clues help us find the answers that are hiding in the text.

Read the passage.

Highlight the reason Theseus was able to escape.

Circle the person King Minos blamed for Theseus' escape.

King Minos was filled with anger. The hero, Theseus, had killed the Minotaur in a labyrinth and had now escaped. The King blamed the master craftsman, Daedalus, for helping Theseus. He ordered that Daedalus be trapped in a tower of the labyrinth he had designed and built, on the island of Crete.

"As extra punishment, your son can join you!" roared King Minos.

Underline how King Minos punished Daedalus.

Colour the extra punishment King Minos meted out to Daedalus.

Circle the correct answers.

1. Which is the best **conclusion**? The Minotaur had been …
   - a imprisoned in the labyrinth.
   - b guarding the prisoners in the labyrinth.
   - c hiding from King Minos.
   - d running away from Theseus.
2. What is the **clue** to question 1's answer?
   - a King Minos imprisoned Daedalus in the labyrinth.
   - b King Minos thought Daedalus had helped Theseus escape.
   - c Theseus was able to escape after killing the Minotaur.
   - d Theseus was a hero.
3. What **conclusion** can we draw about King Minos? King Minos was powerful and …
   - a spiteful.
   - b compassionate.
   - c wise.
   - d merciful.
4. What is the **clue** to question 3's answer? King Minos …
   - a imprisoned Daedalus because he thought he had killed the Minotaur.
   - b imprisoned Daedalus and his son because he thought they were dangerous.
   - c imprisoned Daedalus' son because he thought he would miss his father.
   - d imprisoned Daedalus' innocent son to further punish the master craftsman.

AC9E6LY05 Use comprehension strategies to connect and compare content from a variety of sources

Read the passage.

Circle two things that Daedalus warned could destroy their wings.

Highlight what Daedalus and Icarus had to do to make the wings lift them into the air.

After a year, Daedalus had made two pairs of wings. He strapped one set of wings on himself and the other onto his son.

"Stay close to me, Icarus," said Daedalus. "Listen carefully — do not fly so low that the sea spray soaks the feathers or so high that the sun melts the wax." He showed his son how to flap his arms so the wings beat the air, and together they rose to freedom and away from the tower.

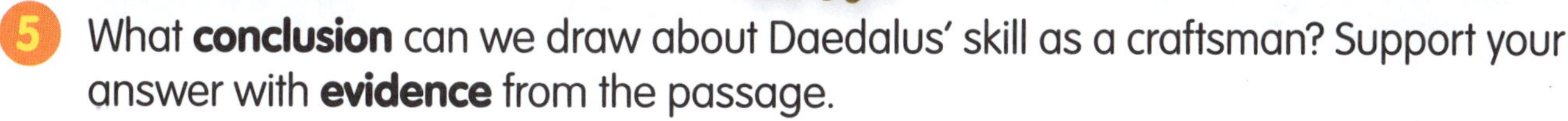

Icarus was excited as the earth fell away, filled with the thrill of flying and finally being free. He began to be careless. Unable to contain his excitement, he flew higher and higher. Icarus completely forgot his father's warning.

Underline the words that suggest that Icarus had not enjoyed being imprisoned.

Colour the words that suggest that Icarus' wings were likely to be destroyed by the sun.

5 What **conclusion** can we draw about Daedalus' skill as a craftsman? Support your answer with **evidence** from the passage.

6 What **conclusion** can we draw about the reliability of the wings Daedalus made? Support your answer with **quotes** from the passage.

7 What **conclusion** can we draw about how Icarus' wings would be destroyed? Support your answer with a **quote** from the passage.

Verb Phrases

A **verb** shows what action is happening and when it happens. A **verb phrase** is a group of words that is built around a **main verb**. For example: **is reading, had fallen, haven't tried, don't slip, can't run**.

Read the extract.

A Safer Place to Hide

In this paragraph, circle three **verb phrases**.

The eye of the storm is passing over us," said Uncle Lou. "We don't have a lot of time. We must go downstairs to the laundry."

In this paragraph, put a box around the **verb phrase**.

"Uncle Lou's right," said Dad. "We can't stay here. If the rest of the house goes, the laundry's our best chance."

In this sentence, highlight two **verb phrases**.

With his torch, Dad led the way out of the bathroom. The inside of the house was a mess. The Christmas tree had blown across the room, and now the tip of it was wedged under the fridge. Broken furniture and glass lay everywhere. All the windows were broken. Everything was wet.

In this paragraph, colour the **verb phrases**.

Uncle Lou was already outside. "Be careful of the stairs, they aren't holding on by much."

Mum carried Baxter and cautiously made her way down.

Circle the correct answers.

Which verb phrase completes the sentence?

1. Mum _____ the cyclone would cause so much trouble.
   a don't think b didn't think c can think d won't think
2. The family _____ any longer.
   a can wait b could wait c couldn't wait d would wait
3. Broken glass _____ everywhere.
   a were lying b are lying c weren't lying d was lying
4. By next morning, the wind _____.
   a has stopped b had stopped c have stopped d is stopping
5. The plants in the yard _____.
   a had been destroyed b was being destroyed c has been destroyed

 AC9E6LA06 Understand how ideas can be expanded and sharpened through careful choice of verbs, elaborated tenses and a range of adverb groups

6 **Complete each sentence with a main verb.**

a We were ______________________ dinner when lightning struck the house.

b By the time we got there, it had ______________________ raining.

c You can ______________________ outside when the weather clears.

d You must ______________________ the windows before the storm gets here.

e He hasn't ______________________ the mud off his rain boots.

7 **Complete each sentence with a verb from the box below.**

a Most tropical cyclones are ____________________ people's names, such as Cyclone Tracy.

b The meteorologist has been ______________________ the weather patterns.

c During the cyclone, all the people could __________ was follow some basic rules.

d Tornadoes _______________ suck up anything from cows to combine harvesters.

e You ____________________ check that the roofs, gutters and eaves are secure.

f You ____________________ want a tornado to twist through your kitchen.

g At least 70% of houses had ____________________ seriously damaged.

do	been	studying	given	don't	should	can

8 **In each sentence, circle the verb phrase.**

a The cyclone had ripped the roof off the house.

b The branches were blowing about in the wind.

c Cyclone Tracy had washed away their presents.

d Entire parts of the city had been destroyed.

e Many families had been left with nothing.

f The evacuation centres were overflowing with people.

g Women and children would be evacuated first.

AC9E6LA06 Understand how ideas can be expanded and sharpened through careful choice of verbs, elaborated tenses and a range of adverb groups

LESSON 216

Out Now!

Compare and Contrast

When we compare and contrast information, we look for the similarities and differences between details in the text.

Read the passage.

Highlight the words that give information about two of the articles for the summer issue.

Circle the words that suggest that there is a feeling of excitement about the summer issue.

As I read through the articles for the summer issue, I notice there's an interesting one on making skateboards and another on secret beach huts that kids have built. Both are great for the summer issue.

There's a huge buzz around the summer issue — and this one is shaping up to be our biggest ever. Our readers and advertisers look forward to it as we always try to do something to make these issues different and collectable. We have a few surprises in the pipeline — which is a good sign.

Putting together this issue can take eight months to plan and organise. This is fairly stressful as we still have to publish the monthly issues of *Hive* in the meantime.

Put a box around the word that suggests that readers like to keep the summer issues.

Colour how long it takes to plan and organise a summer issue.

Underline how often *Hive* is published.

Circle the correct answers.

1. How are the articles on skateboards and secret beach huts that kids have built **similar**?
   - a They are written by the same person.
   - b They contain the same number of words.
   - c Both will be included in the summer issue.
   - d Both are about secret projects.
2. How will the current summer issue be **different** from previous ones? It …
   - a will be more exciting.
   - b contain more advertisements.
   - c will be more interesting.
   - d will be the biggest one yet.
3. What is **similar** about all of the summer issues? The editorial team tries to make each one …
   - a more colourful.
   - b collectable.
   - c longer.
   - d less expensive.
4. How is the summer issue **different** from the monthly issues of *Hive*? It …
   - a takes longer to plan and organise.
   - b contains more photographs.
   - c contains fewer advertisements.
   - d targets a different audience.

AC9E6LY05 Use comprehension strategies to connect and compare content from a variety of sources

Read the passage.

Highlight how the content of early magazines was different from the content of modern magazines.

Underline the description of early magazine covers.

Early magazines did not restrict themselves to leisure interests but often had political and religious content. In the mid-1700s, magazines did not always have what we now see as covers. Many had their cover page as a table of contents, or they began an article on the cover. The first teen magazines appeared in America and England in the 1940s.

There's now a magazine for practically every imaginable interest, from fashion or food, to football or fishing.

There are more magazines today than ever before. Magazines both inform and entertain. It's this magical combination that has kept sales rising for nearly 300 years.

Colour the sentence that suggests that modern magazines cater for all tastes.

Put a box around what the main purpose of magazines has been for the last 300 years.

5 Carefully explain the **differences** between early and modern magazines.

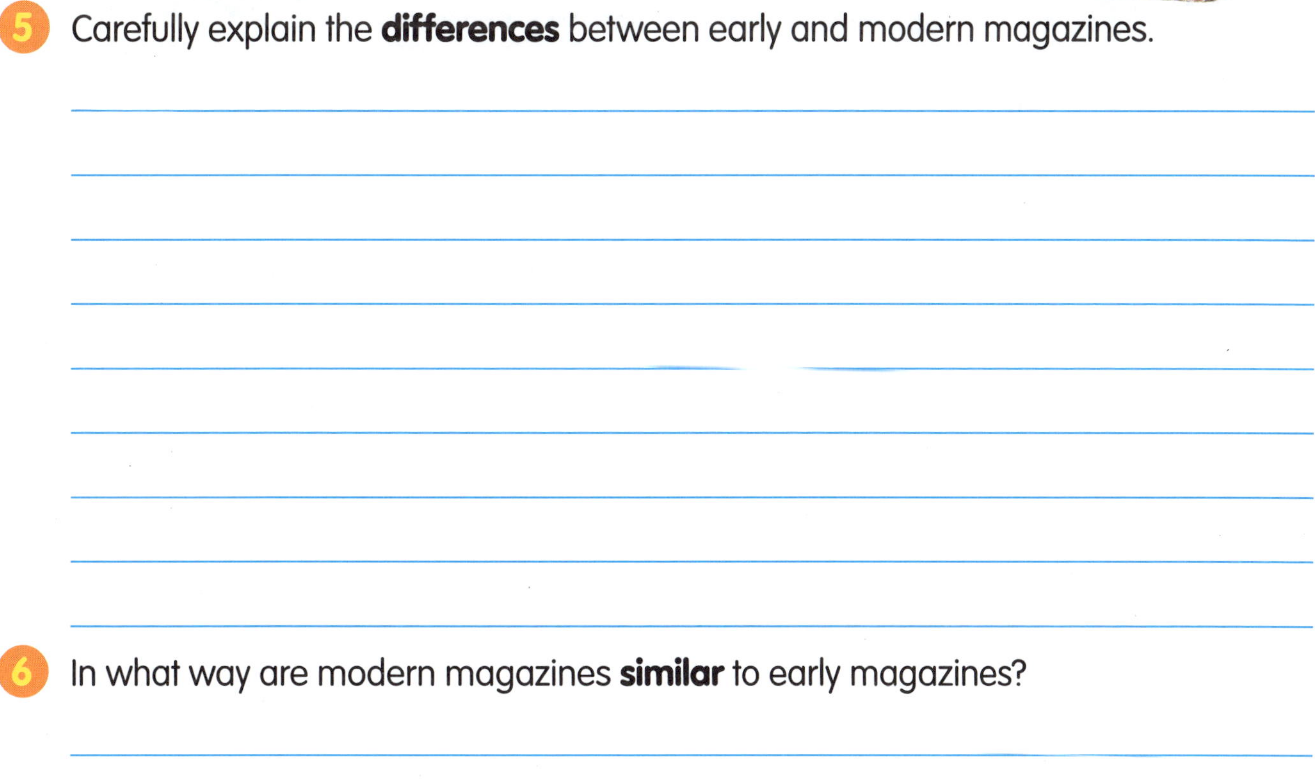

6 In what way are modern magazines **similar** to early magazines?

LESSON 217

Recycling

Sequencing Events

To identify the sequence of events in a text, we usually look at numbers and words that give clues to the order in which things happen.

Read the passage.

Circle the abbreviation for polyethylene terephthalate.

Highlight the first step in the recycling of PET bottles.

Put a box around how PET bottles are sorted.

Plastic stamped with identification code 1 are PET (polyethylene terephthalate) plastics, often used as soft drink, water and juice bottles.

PET bottles are recycled by separating them from other types of plastic, and sorting them into different colour groups: clear, blue and green, and a mixed colour group.

They are then crushed and transported to the recycler.

Once there, they are sorted again, washed and then shredded into flakes. The flakes are washed, dried and melted to make new plastic products: fleece clothing, pillows, carpets, ropes, sleeping bags, life jackets, furniture, building materials—and more PET bottles.

Colour where PET bottles are taken after they have been crushed.

Underline what happens to the flakes before they are made into new plastic products.

Circle the correct answers.

1. Which process happens **first**? PET bottles are …
   - a sorted into different colour groups.
   - b separated from other types of plastic.
   - c transported to the recycler.
   - d shredded into flakes.
2. What happens **before** the PET bottles are taken to the recycler? They are …
   - a shredded.
   - b washed.
   - c melted.
   - d crushed.
3. Which process happens **last**? The PET bottles are …
   - a transported to the recycler.
   - b sorted into different colour groups.
   - c crushed.
   - d separated from other types of plastic.
4. What happens **after** the PET bottles have been shredded into flakes? The flakes are …
   - a sorted.
   - b washed.
   - c crushed.
   - d separated.
5. What is the **final** process before the flakes are made into new plastic products? The flakes are …
   - a melted.
   - b dried.
   - c washed.
   - d sorted.

AC9E6LY05 Use comprehension strategies to build literal and inferred meaning

Read the passage.

Highlight the first step in the recycling process.

Underline what happens after the glass has been sorted.

Circle the name for crushed glass.

Glass for recycling is sorted by colour: clear, amber and green. Materials that contaminate the glass, such as metal bottle tops, are removed.

The glass is crushed into cullet. Cullet is often mixed with the raw materials of glass (sand, soda ash and limestone) before being melted in a furnace at up to 1500° Celsius.

The molten glass is poured into moulding machines and air is blown through it to shape new glass products. These are cooled down slowly before they can be used.

Put a box around the temperature at which the glass is melted.

Colour how new glass products are made.

6 Complete the following sentences so that they show the correct sequence for recycling glass.

a The first step in the recycling of glass is to ______________________________

____

b After that, ____

____

____

c Once the foreign materials have been removed, ______________________________

____

d The cullet is then melted. This is done by ______________________________

____

____

e To produce new glass products, ______________________________

____

____

f The final step ____

____

Conservation

Drawing Conclusions

To draw conclusions from a text, we have to use clues to make our own judgements. The clues help us find the answers that are hiding in the text.

Read the passage.

Circle the different types of fossil fuels.

Highlight a way that power companies can make burning coal a cleaner process.

Underline the reason power companies use "scrubbers".

Almost all of our electricity comes from burning fossil fuels: coal, natural gas and oil. Power companies can make burning coal a cleaner process by washing coal before burning it. They can also burn a type of coal that contains less pollution-producing sulphur, or use devices called "scrubbers" to remove sulphur dioxide from the gas that leaves the power plant.

Individuals can also have a major effect on reducing pollution. People can use less electricity and choose "green power" — electricity that comes from non-polluting sources, such as hydro-electricity and wind farms.

Colour a way that individuals can reduce pollution.

Underline what is meant by "green power".

Put a box around two sources of "green power".

Circle the correct answers.

1. Which is the best **conclusion**?
   - a All power companies use "scrubbers".
   - b Some coal contains sulphur.
   - c All coal contains sulphur.
   - d Some coal does not cause pollution.
2. Which group of words is the best **clue** to question 1's answer?
   - a less pollution-producing sulphur
   - b use devices called "scrubbers"
   - c washing coal before burning it
   - d gas that leaves the power plant
3. Based on evidence in the passage, which is the best **conclusion**?
   - a Wind is a non-renewable energy source.
   - b Wind farms cause air pollution.
   - c Wind is a non-polluting energy source.
   - d Wind farms are expensive to run.
4. Which group of words is the **clue** to question 3's answer?
   - a less electricity
   - b a major effect
   - c green power
   - d reducing pollution
5. From evidence in the passage, which **conclusion** can we draw about burning coal? It is …
   - a a cheap way to produce electricity.
   - b a clean way to produce electricity.
   - c the most efficient way to produce electricity.
   - d bad for the environment.

AC9E6LY05 Use comprehension strategies to connect and compare content from a variety of sources

Read the passage.

Highlight the prediction scientists have made about global warming.

Put a box around how changes to the environment could affect people.

Circle the word that shows that it is not easy to predict the exact effects of global warming.

Scientists predict that global warming will cause massive changes to the environment. These changes will affect everyone — where they live, how they travel and the cost of living.

It is difficult to predict the exact effects of global warming. How quickly the climate will change depends on how much greenhouse gas emissions grow, and how sensitive the climate is to these emissions.

Extremes of weather have been predicted — more frequent and intense heatwaves, storms, floods and droughts. Farms would yield fewer crops. Rising ocean levels, from melting ice caps, could force millions of people from their homes.

Colour the extremes of weather that are expected to result from global warming.

Underline how global warming could affect our food supply.

Highlight the reason people could be forced from their homes.

6 From reading the passage, we can **conclude** that global warming is a huge problem. What **evidence** is there in the text to **support** this statement?

LESSON 219

HMS Endeavour Strikes the Great Barrier Reef

Making Connections

Linking a text to other texts you have read is a great way to build understanding. Look for key words and phrases in the texts to make the connections.

Read the passages.

Journal entry of Joseph Banks — 11 June 1770

... the tide ebbed so much that we found it impossible to attempt to get [the ship] off till next high water, if she would hold together so long; and we now found to add to our misfortune that we had got ashore nearly at the top of high water and as night tides generally rise higher than day ones we had little hopes of getting off even then.

Circle the date of each journal entry.

In both texts, **highlight** what happened to the ship.

In Banks's text, underline the words that suggest when the incident occurred.

In Captain Cook's text, underline where the ship came to rest.

Journal entry of Captain James Cook — 11 June 1770

Before 10 o'clock we had 20 and 21 fathoms, and continued in that depth until a few minutes before 11, when we had 17, and before the man at the lead could heave another cast, the ship struck and stuck fast. Immediately upon this we took in all our sails, hoisted out the boats and sounded round the ship, and found that we had got upon the south-east edge of a reef of coral rocks.

Circle the correct answers.

1. What information do both texts give the reader about the events of 11 June 1770? The ship ...
   - **a** was breaking up.
   - **b** had run aground.
   - **c** was lying at anchor.
   - **d** was sinking.

2. What extra information does Captain Cook give the reader about the incident? The ship had ...
   - **a** hit a sand bar.
   - **b** drifted off course.
   - **c** lost a mast.
   - **d** struck a coral reef.

3. How is Joseph Banks's account of the incident different from Captain Cook's?
   - **a** It contains personal opinions.
   - **b** It contains more nautical terms.
   - **c** It contains only facts.
   - **d** It recounts the events in chronological order.

4. What information do both texts give the reader about when the incident occurred? It occurred ...
   - **a** in the morning.
   - **b** in the afternoon.
   - **c** at night.
   - **d** at noon.

AC9E6LY05 Use comprehension strategies to connect and compare content from a variety of sources

Read the passages.

Joseph Banks's journal entry

Orders were now given for lightening the ship, which began by starting our water and pumping it up; the ballast was then got up and thrown over board, as well as 6 of our guns (all that we had upon deck).

At night the tide almost floated her but she made water so fast that three pumps hard worked could but just keep her clear. Now, in my own opinion I entirely gave up the ship and, packing up what I thought I might save, prepared myself for the worst.

In both texts, **highlight** how the sailors made the ship lighter.

Underline the extra information Joseph Banks gives about the guns.

Colour how Joseph Banks felt about their situation.

Captain Cook's journal entry

As we went ashore about the top of high water we not only started water, but threw overboard our guns, iron and stone ballast, casks, hoop staves, oil jars, decayed stores, etc.; many of these last articles lay in the way at coming at heavier. All this time the ship made little or no water. At 11 am, being high water as we thought, we tried to heave her off without success, she not being afloat by a foot or more, notwithstanding by this time we had thrown overboard 40 or 50 tonnes of weight.

5 From reading both texts, what does the reader learn about the measures taken to float the ship?

6 Which text gives a more personal account of the incident? Give reasons for your answer.

Ready for Take-off

Reading Diagrams

Diagrams and pictures are often used to explain scientific or technical ideas. They help us understand the text by representing information in a visual form.

Study the text.

Circle the correct answers.

1. What is the main purpose of the pictures in the above text? The pictures show what the aircraft mentioned in the text …
   a can do. b are used for. c look like.
2. Which picture shows a helicopter? Picture number …
   a 1 b 2 c 3 d 4
3. Which picture shows a military aircraft? Picture number …
   a 1 b 2 c 3 d 4
4. Which aircraft pictured above is the most basic type of aircraft?
   a the microlight b the military aircraft c the helicopter d the light aircraft

AC9E6LA07 Identify and explain how images, figures, tables, diagrams, maps and graphs contribute to meaning

Study the text.

Colour the word that means *height above ground or sea level.*

Highlight another name for an attitude indicator.

Aircraft have instruments to provide the pilot with important information.

Basic aircraft instruments include:

- airspeed indicator — indicates how fast the plane is moving through the air
- altimeter — indicates the altitude of the aircraft, above the ground or above sea level
- attitude indicator — also called an *artificial horizon*, indicates the exact orientation of the plane as it pitches and rolls through the air.

Modern aeroplanes have lots of instruments to keep track of!

Keeping yourself the right way up – even when you can't see anything!

Colour the images of aeroplanes.

Place a ✔ beside the pilot whose stripes show that he has the higher rank.

5 Carefully explain how the pictures of aircraft instruments add to the reader's understanding of the text.

____

____

____

6 If there were no text to accompany the pictures, how would the reader know that the pictures are of aircraft instruments?

____

____

____

7 What do the pictures suggest about the number of pilots required to fly a large passenger plane?

____

____

AC9E6LA07 Identify and explain how images, figures, tables, diagrams, maps and graphs contribute to meaning

The Future Tense

The most common ways of showing future time are by combining **will** or **be going to** with the main verb. For example: **They will arrive soon. We'll see you later. It won't happen. I'm going to meet them there.** **Will** can also be combined with **be** and **have**. For example: **They will be waiting for us. They will have gone by then.**

Read the extract.

In paragraph 3, circle four **verb phrases** that express actions that will happen in the future.

In the final paragraph, put a box around two **verb phrases** that express actions that will happen in the future.

Robots to the Rescue

Nanorobots, or nanobots, are very, very small robots—smaller than the width of a human hair.

Nanobots are still in the development stage. They are expected to revolutionise the way doctors treat diseases.

In the future, scientists believe that doctors will inject nanobots into our blood. The nanobots will swim through our bodies, looking for signs of illness. If, for instance, they detect a virus, they will destroy it before it makes us sick. In addition, these little helpers will give us medicine when we need it.

Some scientists are even predicting that in the future, people won't grow old. As soon as our cells show signs of wear and tear, nanobots will replace them with healthy ones.

Circle the correct answers.

In each sentence, identify the verb that shows future time.

1. Scientists think that nanorobots will exist in the not too distant future.
   a think that b will exist c not too distant d distant future

2. Scientists are developing nanorobots that will change the way doctors treat illnesses.
   a are developing b treat illnesses c doctors treat d will change

3. By the time I grow up, doctors will be treating patients with nanobots.
   a I grow b grow up c will be d will be treating

4. Scientists predict that robots will be playing a bigger role in our lives in the future.
   a predict that b will be c be playing d will be playing

5. Some scientists believe that nanobots are going to wipe out all diseases.
   a are going b believe that c are going to wipe out d to wipe

 AC9E6LA06 Understand how ideas can be expanded and sharpened through careful choice of verbs, elaborated tenses and a range of adverb groups

6 **In each sentence, fill in the gap with an auxiliary verb.**

- **a** In the future, robots ____________ be able to do more jobs around the house.
- **b** This week, my mother ____________ going to buy a robotic vacuum cleaner.
- **c** In ten years, some robots will ____________ able to do things we have never imagined.
- **d** This week in science, I ____________ going to help my friend build a robot.
- **e** Do you think robots ____________ ever be able to do our homework for us?

7 **Complete each sentence with a verb phrase from the box below.**

- **a** Robots of the future ____________________ small enough to go right inside our bodies.
- **b** We ____ to a talk about nanobots.
- **c** Nanobots ______________________________ the way diseases are treated.
- **d** Eventually, many of the jobs that humans do ____________________________ by robots.
- **e** The robots ______________________________________ with computer brains.
- **f** Some people are worried that one day, robots ____________________________ the world.
- **g** By the time I grow up, scientists ____________________________________ the first nanobots.

will have built	**are going to listen**	**will be fitted**	**will be done**
will change	**will be**	**will take over**	

8 **Complete each sentence.**

- **a** I believe that nanobots are going to ____________________________________

  ____

- **b** Do you think nanobots will ____

  ____

- **c** With nanobots in our blood, people will ______________________________

  ____

ASSESSMENT 4:

Should Zoos Take Gorillas out of Their Natural Environment?

Lexile: 1170L

There are three subspecies of gorilla living in Africa—the western lowland, eastern lowland and mountain gorilla—and all are endangered. While people generally feel that something must be done to prevent gorillas from becoming extinct, they have different views on how this should happen.

Some people believe that the only way to prevent gorillas from becoming extinct is to remove them from their natural environment and protect them in zoos. They use the following arguments to support their point of view.

Firstly, not only are gorilla numbers dwindling, but gorillas also have a slow rate of reproduction. If more gorillas were kept in zoos, modern medical procedures such as in-vitro fertilisation could be used to increase gorilla numbers. In 1995, for example, a cooperative project between two zoos using in-vitro fertilisation and embryo transfer resulted in the birth of a lowland gorilla baby.

Secondly, the lifespan of gorillas in the wild is 30–40 years. In captivity it is 40–50 years. As zoos continue to research these primates and learn more about their ideal living conditions, their lifespans could increase further.

Finally, some believe that gorilla tourism in the wild is causing gorillas to get human borne infections and diseases. One gorilla group in the Bwindi Impenetrable National Park in Uganda recently suffered an outbreak of scabies. Over half of its population died. In a controlled zoological environment, diseases can be prevented or treated.

However, there are people who are against zoos taking gorillas out of their natural environment. They believe that gorilla conservation programs are a more effective way of protecting these animals. They argue that in the wild, gorillas eat 200 types of leaves, fungus, fruit and even some insects. Replicating this range of food in a zoo is almost impossible. They also cite the fact that gorillas are nomadic and have a home range of up to 24 square kilometres.

Looking at both sides of the argument, it appears that while zoos cannot reproduce the natural environment of gorillas, it is important that at least some are kept in captivity so that they can continue to breed.

Circle the correct answer for each question.

1 Which subspecies of gorilla is in danger of becoming extinct? **LITERAL**

a the western lowland gorilla　　b the eastern lowland gorilla

c the mountain gorilla　　d all of them

2 What do most people agree about? Gorillas must … LITERAL

a be protected in zoos.
b be left in the wild.
c be saved from extinction.
d eat a balanced diet.

3 What are the TWO most likely reasons gorillas live longer in captivity? In captivity, gorillas … CRITICAL

a have a constant supply of food.
b get more exercise.
c have no predators.
d have better shelters.

4 Which sentence is true? Gorillas in the wild eat … INFERENTIAL

a mainly fruit.
b mainly insects.
c a varied diet.
c a diet low in nutrients.

5 Why does the writer think some gorillas should be kept in zoos? LITERAL

a to keep them safe
b to help educate people about them
c to help increase their numbers
d to treat their diseases

6 Which is the odd word out? VOCABULARY

a dwindling
b increasing
c decreasing
d shrinking

7 Which sentence is NOT supported by evidence in the text? INFERENTIAL

a Zoos sometimes work together.
b Gorillas are native to Africa.
c Gorillas are happier in zoos.
d Uganda is in Africa.

8 What is the main purpose of this text? CRITICAL

a to tell a story
b to discuss both sides of an argument
c to recount a series of events
d to explain how something works

9 Where can people see live gorillas? LITERAL

____

____

10 Why would it be impossible to replicate a gorilla's natural diet in a zoo? CRITICAL

____

____

Lesson 181

Pg 2

Sipu made walking through the jungle look easy. It wasn't scary with Sipu around. This was his home. He had grown up here. Sipu thought nothing of climbing over tree roots double his height, breaking vines for a quick drink and climbing up a tree for a bite to eat. He walked so lightly through the forest his feet barely marked the ground. He showed Mia and Flynn how to walk through the rainforest without being seen or heard.

1 a **2** c **3** b **4** b **5** c

Pg 3

"Hey, look guys!" cried Flynn, pointing to the sky. It was dark now and the moon sat full in the night sky. It looked strangely golden. "Doesn't that look awesome?"

The strange coloured moonlight was making them all look golden. El Dorado was with them. Flynn and Mia thought about Sipu and his secret tribe and the great gift that he had given them. He had shown them some of the real treasures of the rainforest, and they would keep their word and do whatever they could to protect it. Their visit to El Dorado would remain a treasured secret forever.

6 Flynn says the moon looks awesome. This tells us he is impressed and inspired by it.

7 Flynn and Mia respect the rainforest— "do whatever they could to protect it".

8 Flynn and Mia think El Dorado is a special place. They do not want people to know about it. It is a "treasured secret".

Lesson 182

Pg 4

When Nick gets home from school, Dad and Mum are sitting chatting at the kitchen table. "Not working, Dad?" he asks, noticing the mugs of tea and packet of biscuits.

"I knocked off early to give Mum a hand moving furniture at Sunset Heights. It's Mrs Blessop's ninetieth birthday party tomorrow," Dad explains.

"Will you lend a hand too, Nick? There are a dozen trestle tables to be shifted," Mum asks when he sits down at the table.

Nick sighs. "Yeah, I'll help."

1 b **2** d **3** b **4** a **5** c

Pg 5

Nick walks to Sunset Heights the long way. His feet are in charge and just happen to be taking him this way.

When he gets to Laura Fleming's house, Nick scans the large garden with its manicured lawns, tall trees and rose beds. There's a Saab parked on the gravel drive and also a new, red SUV. Nick notices a couple of builders mixing concrete near the front steps.

Nick thinks of his dad, who works hard every day, but doesn't seem to get very much— just a boring little house and not much else.

6 Nick blames his feet for taking the long route, which suggests that he wanted to take the long way all along.

7 The Flemings are wealthy and have nice, expensive things.

8 He compares his house to the Flemings' house. He says his dad works hard but they live in "a boring little house".

Lesson 183

Pg 6

They were spinning out of the marketplace and out of control.

"Ouch! Ouch! Ouch!" yelped Flynn, peeling Curiosity off his head. "Watch your claws, you dumb cat. Let go! Mia, move your elbow—it's breaking my ribs." Mia struggled to her feet. They had landed in bushes, on a dune behind a beach.

Hearing voices, they fell silent. They crawled to the top of the dune and peered over.

1 d **2** c **3** d **4** a **5** c

Pg 7

Oak Island is a small island off the coast of Nova Scotia, Canada. Legend says that treasure is buried in a pit on the island. In 1795, a teenager called Daniel McGinnis uncovered what he believed to be a site for buried treasure. With the help of friends he began to dig. They were forced to abandon their search, however, because the hole kept filling with water.

Over the next 200 years many different groups tried to find what was hidden in the pit. All the things uncovered so far are thought to be clues to bigger treasure—coins, gold chains, parchment and a stone with strange writing.

6 There is evidence of buried treasure on Oak Island—"coins, gold chains, parchment and a stone with strange writing" have been uncovered.

7 The items uncovered so far suggest that the treasure could be ancient and valuable. The strange writing suggests that there is something mysterious about it.

Lesson 184

Pg 8

Now folksies, tonight we are giving you a new feature—an extra service. Ladies and gentlemen of our vast unconscious audience, you have heard of jokes funny enough to make a horse laugh—well, that's the kind of jokes we want on this program, jokes funny enough to make a horse laugh, and in carrying out our policy of service to the people, beginning tonight we are bringing a horse into the studio to try our jokes out on. What other radio station would go to such lengths for its public?

1 c **2** b **3** d **4** a

Pg 9

[Hoofs fade in. Note, use wooden hoofs.]

Come here, Molasses—whoa—whoa—all ready for work?

[Snort]

Good! Now, Molasses, I am going to tell you a joke.

[Snort and run away.]

Hey bring that horse back here!

[Hoof in.]

Whoa! Molasses, you misunderstood me.

[Snort]

5 "whoa" and "hey"

6 The text contains script directions and dialogue.

7 Sound effects are used to help the audience imagine the action.

Lesson 185

Pg 10

Long ago in the Dreamtime, Kangaroo did not have a tail. He was good friends with Wombat and they both lived in huts built from tree bark.

At night, Kangaroo liked to sleep outside where he could look up at the stars. He made fun of Wombat for always wanting to sleep inside the hut.

When winter came, Kangaroo still slept outside and teased Wombat about his smelly hut. But one night, rain fell so hard that each drop felt like a jab by a spear on Kangaroo's back. Kangaroo struggled against the wind to reach Wombat's hut. "Let me in!" he cried.

1 c **2** b **3** d

Pg 11

Kangaroo lay in the corner. There was a hole in the wall, where wind and rain came in. He couldn't get dry or warm, and he grew angry as he watched Wombat enjoying a dream.

In the morning, Kangaroo was stiff and sore. He hobbled outside and picked up a large rock. He dropped the rock on Wombat's head, flattening his forehead and making his nose curl around.

Wombat planned his revenge. He waited until Kangaroo was busy washing and then he threw a spear at him. The spear landed at the base of Kangaroo's spine. Kangaroo tried to pull the spear out, but it was stuck.

"From now on, that will be your tail," yelled Wombat.

4 **a** there was a hole in the wall where the wind and rain came in.
b he dropped a rock on Wombat's head, flattening his forehead and making his nose curl around.
c throwing a spear at Kangaroo while we was washing.
d it became his tail.

Grammar Lesson 1

Pg 12

Almost Twins

People said they were sorry about the fire, but that the Khans were very lucky to have escaped. They began discussing plans for a new, much bigger shop.

In the afternoon, Lela made her delicious coconut sponge with pink icing, and in the evening, the families gathered to sing "Happy Birthday" to Adi and Priya.

Finally, when all the village girls and women lined up on the lawn for their famous Fijian fan dance, Priya joined them. She was dressed in a brightly coloured sarong and grass skirt and held a beautifully woven fan. It was her birthday present from Adi.

"We are so fortunate to have such wonderful daughters, aren't we?" said Agnessi Kinitavaki, putting her arm around Lela Khan and squeezing hard.

1 c **2** b **3** d **4** a **5** c

Pg 13

6 **a** more delicious than this
b of very strong tea **c** of very difficult steps
d beautifully woven **e** of the shop
f of crimson flames

7 **a** chocolate cakes decorated with icing
b birthday parties with lots of presents
c red sparks from the fire
d exciting plans for the future
e large groups of happy people

8 **a** very excited **b** beautiful, handmade
c far too much **d** brightly coloured
e exactly the same age

Lesson 186

Pg 14

Most of the water we use comes from rivers, lakes or dams.

A river starts from melting ice, rainfall or from a lake, and grows as streams in its catchment area join it.

An important source of fresh water is ground water. The water collects above a layer of rock that is too dense to allow it to flow through. People dig wells to bring this water to the surface again. Around the world, ground water is the most accessible source of fresh water—about 1.5 billion people use it for their drinking water.

1 b **2** d **3** a **4** c

Pg 15

Drinking water is water that is safe for people to drink and to use for cooking, washing and bathing. Water is cleaned and purified before it is ready to drink.

Water is pumped from a river, lake or dam into a tank. A chemical called alum is added to the water so that impurities coagulate into small particles called flocs.

The water is then transferred into a sedimentation tank. The flocs attract dirt and sink to the bottom as sediment. The clear water above the sediment is pumped to the next stage, filtration.

5 **a** made pure **b** harmful things
c to clot or thicken
d solid materials at the bottom of a liquid
e the process of removing unwanted materials

Lesson 187

Pg 16

Marc-Antoine Careme (1784–1833) was considered the master of French cooking, creating dishes that often looked more like sculptures. He cooked for royalty and the rich and famous. His cuisine was the talk of Europe.

Via his travels, Careme introduced to France such delicacies as caviar (unfertilised fish eggs) and *pashka* (a creamy Russian cheesecake).

While in England, he produced a jellied custard set in a crown of ladyfingers (long, thin biscuits). He named it the Charlotte Russe—a pastry still baked today.

Careme also prepared massive feasts. At one military festival, he served 10 000 guests from a menu that required 6 cows, 75 calves, 250 sheep, 8000 turkeys, 2000 chickens, 1000 partridges, 500 hams and 2000 fish.

1 a **2** b, c, d

Pg 17

A kitchen is designed like a factory—raw materials (ingredients) come in at one end of the production line and exit at the other end as a meal ready to be served.

Kitchens are divided into clearly defined areas, called stations, that handle different tasks. Because a kitchen is a busy and sometimes dangerous environment, it is organised to make it easy to work in and move around. For example, wait staff and kitchen staff meet where dishes are served and dirty plates collect, but otherwise keep out of each other's way.

3 The way in which a large commercial kitchen is organised and operates.

4 "A kitchen is designed like a factory." "Kitchens are divided into clearly defined areas." "A kitchen is organised to make it easy to work in and move around."

Lesson 188

Pg 18

Polar bears live mainly on ice floes in the Arctic. They are not endangered now, but they are considered at risk and in need of conservation.

Polar bears have been hunted for thousands of years by the native Inuit people who share their habitat. Inuit people use polar bear fur for clothing and the meat and fat for food. They kill only what they need to survive.

Sport hunters began using aircraft and motor boats to hunt polar bears. As a result, bear numbers have declined.

1 b **2** d **3** a **4** d

Pg 19

In the last 500 years, humans have forced 844 species to extinction. Will we ever stop?

Chimpanzees are one of the species in danger. They are our closest relative in the animal world, sharing an estimated 98 percent of our genes. Chimpanzees are highly intelligent and show emotions like happiness and sadness, fear and love. Yet, humans threaten their future.

Urgent action is necessary to protect the remaining chimpanzee populations.

5 The author is critical of the way humans treat animals—"humans have forced 844 species to extinction".

6 The author uses a rhetorical question—"Will we ever stop?" The author gives statistics—"humans have forced 844 species to extinction". The author appeals to the reader's emotions—uses words like "happiness", "sadness" to compare chimps to humans.

7 The author feels very strongly—"Urgent action is necessary".

Lesson 189

Pg 20

Text 1	Text 2
The site plan of the new development on the city's edge has sparked a firestorm of debate. The plan includes a staggering number of standard office, retail and apartment buildings, which seem to grow taller with every new glossy brochure that the developer produces. But it is not like the city is filled with beautiful architecture that this new waterfront development will somehow "spoil".	A proposal to build 20-storey office and apartment towers across a section of the harbour has become a topic of heated debate. On the one hand, there are those who argue that the city can expand in one direction only—upwards. Others, however, believe that too many tall buildings along the water's edge will spoil the look and feel of the city's greatest asset—its beautiful, meandering waterway.

1 **a** Both texts **b** Both texts **c** Text 1
d Both texts **e** Text 1 **f** Text 2
g Text 1

Pg 21

Text 1	Text 2
We do have a beautiful city, but it relies heavily on its natural charms, rather than what we've built in it. If we are to see our city grow and change, let's be brave and embrace what the world's best architects are offering. If we are not careful, this development could turn into yet another maze of concrete canyons which rarely see sunshine. Loudly expressed public opinion could make all the difference.	The plans for the new development on the waterfront fill me with dismay. Are our city planners really going to allow this section of the harbour to become just another concrete jungle? Surely there are architects out there who can come up with more creative and exciting plans for the area! I urge those of you who feel as I do to stand up and make your voices heard!

2 They feel that the new development contains too many tall, boring buildings—"a maze of concrete canyons", "another concrete jungle".

3 They encourage ordinary citizens to express their disapproval of the new development and insist on more "creative and exciting plans".

Lesson 190

Pg 22

Space settlements are enclosed areas in orbit. Scientists believe that people will live in these settlements sometime in the future.

Space settlements could be in the shape of a sphere, cylinder or even a doughnut, but they must be airtight, so they maintain air pressure and a breathable atmosphere. They must also rotate in order to create artificial gravity.

Space settlements need constant sunlight to produce solar power. They also need some sort of barrier to protect them from the Sun's radiation. On Earth, our atmosphere provides this protection. Later settlements may decide to leave our solar system, but they will still need protection from the radiation of other stars.

1 **a** F **b** O **c** F **d** F **e** F **f** F **g** F **h** O

Pg 23

People living in space may still want regular contact and visits with Earth. Therefore, spacecraft launches from both Earth and the settlement will need to be cheap. An environmentally-safe method of launching craft from Earth needs to be invented, due to the risk to the Earth's atmosphere from a large number of launches.

NASA has studied the possibility of building space settlements in orbit. They believe it is possible, as plenty of the necessary materials are available on the Moon or on asteroids. The sun could supply the necessary energy. NASA believes no new scientific breakthroughs are necessary, but lots of engineering would be required.

2 People living in space may still want regular contact and visits with Earth.

3 A large number of launches poses a risk to the Earth's atmosphere.

4 NASA believes that it is possible that one day people will live in space.

5 NASA bases its opinion on the fact that the necessary materials are available on the moon or on asteroids.

Grammar Lesson 2

Pg 24

The Atom

Everything in the world is made up of atoms. They are the main building blocks of matter.

Atoms are made up of three parts—neutrons, protons and electrons. The nucleus—the centre of the atom—is made from neutrons and protons. The electrons orbit the nucleus, just like the planets orbit our sun.

Protons have a positive electrical charge; electrons have a negative charge.

When a positive electrical charge comes into contact with a negative charge, they are attracted to each other. This is what happens with electrons and protons. Alternatively, two things with the same electrical charge repel each other. An atom normally has the same number of protons and electrons—their opposite electrical charges balance each other and make the atom stable.

1 d 2 b 3 d 4 a 5 b

Pg 25

6 insert the ^ between the following words
- a time in
- b unique it
- c atoms quarks
- d quarks up
- e atoms they
- f direction upwards

7
- a Solids are made of densely packed atoms; atoms have gases that are spread out.
- b The electron always has a negative charge; the proton always has a positive charge.
- c A normal atom has a neutral charge; it has equal numbers of positive and negative charges.
- d Neutrons aren't positive or negative; they have a neutral charge.
- e Ice becomes water when it is heated; water becomes ice when it is cooled to 0° Celsius or lower.

8 Everything in the universe—from us to the largest stars—is made up of elements. Compounds are the result of two or more different elements joining together. Some common examples of compounds are salt and sugar. Salt is made up of sodium and chlorine; sugar is made up of carbon, hydrogen and oxygen.

Assessment 1

Pg 26–27

1 b 2 c 3 c 4 b 5 a 6 c 7 b 8 c
9 Teacher check 10 Teacher check

Lesson 191

Pg 28

On the Friday before he left, we gave Mr Sams a surprise farewell party. It wasn't really a surprise because he saw us carrying the party things to school.

It was almost time to go when the principal, Mr Jones, came into our classroom to tell us a new teacher would start on Monday.

On Monday morning, I dragged myself out of bed again. "Another fun day," I thought, wishing I could change places with my older brother, Joel.

"You might get a nice surprise, Andy," Mum said as she packed my lunch. "You might even like this new teacher."

1 b 2 a 3 c 4 b

Pg 29

The next morning I gathered a big armful of roses from Mum's garden. I wrapped them in some cellophane left over from my birthday.

I was going to give them to Miss Thompson in the parking lot, but I changed my mind at the last minute. What if someone saw me? I'd look like a dork. Instead, I slipped into the classroom before the bell rang and put them on her desk.

When Miss Thompson saw them, she couldn't have looked happier. "What a beautiful bunch of roses!" she exclaimed. "Someone in this class must have guessed that they are my favourite flower. I love them! Who was the kind person who brought them in?"

Everybody looked around the room. Of course nobody answered. I wanted to say it was me, but I couldn't. Not in front of everyone!

5
- a picked a bunch of roses from Mum's garden
- b on Miss Thompson's desk.
- c very happy to see the roses.
- d who had brought them in.

Lesson 192

Pg 30

Elizabeth Hammond has a busy life. Much busier than the average eleven-year-old. Elizabeth has a brother, James, aged eight—'a space-occupying lesion'; another brother aged five, called Ted—'sweet but useless'; twin sisters Harriet and Lucy, aged twenty-two months—'still in nappies'; and a father called Jim who spends all day in the attic, except for mealtimes—'trying to write a bestseller'. That is the Hammond family.

1 a 2 c 3 b 4 d 5 c

Pg 31

Elizabeth can't see her knees in the mountain of bubbles and wet clothes. She looks at Heather Shambles and says quietly, "You put the dirty laundry in the dishwasher."

Elizabeth hears her voice trembling. In this crazy moment she wonders whether to cry or shout. Instead, she sits down amongst the bubbles and laughs.

"At least I didn't put the plates in the washing machine," mutters Heather Shambles.

Elizabeth rolls around the kitchen floor, laughing and squealing and kicking her feet in the air. Finally, when she lies quite still, she notices everyone is staring at her. Heather Shambles, Ted, Harriet, Lucy, James—and her father.

6 a mountain of bubbles and wet clothes
7 in the dishwasher
8 She starts rolling around the kitchen floor, laughing and squealing and kicking her feet in the air.
9 Heather Shambles, Ted, Harriet, Lucy, James and Elizabeth's father

Lesson 193

Pg 32

As I went strolling one evening,
Not meaning to go very far,
I spied a pretty young damsel,
Parading her wares at an inn,
A watch she took from a customer,
And she slipped it right in my hand,
And the law came and put me in prison,
Bad luck to her black velvet band.

Chorus

Her eyes shone like the diamonds,
You'd think she was Queen of the land,
And her hair hung over her shoulder,
Tied up with a black velvet band.

1 b 2 c 3 a 4 d 5 b

Pg 33

Next morning before judge and jury,
For trial I had to appear,
And the judge said "Me fine young fellow
The case against you is quite clear,
For seven long years is your sentence,
You're going to Van Diemen's Land,
Away from your friends and relations,
To follow the black velvet band."

Chorus

Her eyes shone like the diamonds,
You'd think she was Queen of the land,
And her hair hung over her shoulder,
Tied up with a black velvet band.

6 The song was written to mainly entertain, but also to show how harshly an innocent man was treated.

7 One evening a young man was out walking. As he passed an inn, a young girl with shinning eyes and hair tied up with a black velvet band, slipped a stolen watch into his hand. He was arrested for robbery. A jury found him guilty, and the judge sentenced him to seven years in Van Diemen's Land.

Lesson 194

Pg 34

I look cool
in these glasses
in the mirror
I am tinted
smooth
slick

Natalie said
my old glasses
made me look like
a bogong moth
big black orbs
instead of eyes

1 d 2 a 3 d 4 a

Pg 35

Natalie said
my old glasses
made me look like
a bogong moth
big black orbs
instead of eyes

now I'm cool
lizard cool
beetle cool
cool insect
that's me.

5
- a a metaphor
- b It is a direct comparison. The poet does not use "like" or "as".

6 The poet's description of herself in her new sunglasses is more flattering. A Bogong moth is ugly—it has eyes like "big black orbs". How she feels "cool", which suggests that she thinks she looks more stylish and fashionable.

Lesson 195

Pg 36

A long time ago, lorikeets not only repeated what a person said, they also spoke their own thoughts.

That was until a man who owned a magnificent lorikeet stole his neighbour's water buffalo. When the neighbour asked if the man knew anything about it, he lied and said, "I have no idea."

But the lorikeet knew the truth. It called out, "Brrk! Master stole it! Master killed it! Master ate part and hid the rest in the rice bins. Brrk!"

1 c **2** d, f **3** a
4 **a** stole **b** hid **c** gobbled
5 c

Pg 37

The guilty man went free. He left the bird, wanting never to see it again. The lorikeet flew back to the jungle, where it met a new bird, the parrot. The lorikeet looked at the parrot's wonderful colours and knew that, one day, man would want it for a pet. The lorikeet warned the parrot, "Brrt! Do not speak your own mind to people! You will get into a lot of trouble. Repeat only what they say. They love to hear their own thoughts."

Today, the parrot remembers the lorikeet's warning, and this is why it only repeats what people say.

6 "guilty"
7 He abandoned the lorikeet.
8 "wonderful colours"
9 "trouble"
10 They love to hear their own thoughts.

Grammar Lesson 3

Pg 38

Tom's Ambition

Tom had ambition. He wanted to be Prime Minister when he grew up.

Another thing Tom wanted was a fish. That was why he was at the pet shop staring at the fish tanks. He had been saving his pocket money for weeks and now he finally had enough.

But while Tom had been staring at the fish, a ferret had been eyeing him. Now it tried to get his attention. "Psst!" it said.

Tom turned around, but no-one was there.

"What's the matter with you, Kid?" said the ferret. "You must have bananas in your ears. Can't you hear when someone is talking to you?"

The ferret was in a cage near Tom. It was standing on its hind legs, with its paws resting on the bars of its cage. It was looking straight at Tom with beady little eyes.

1 d **2** c **3** a **4** b **5** c

Pg 39

6 Teacher check
7 **a** have/had **b** has/had **c** has/have or had **d** have/had **e** have/has or had
8 **a** has been finding **b** has been trying **c** has been selling **d** have been helping **e** has been meaning **f** has been listening

Lesson 196

Pg 40

There is very little gravity in orbit, so it is known as microgravity. This means things are done differently from the way they are done on Earth.

Food is mainly dehydrated or heat-stabilised. Drinks are also dehydrated. Once food has been rehydrated and heated, astronauts eat the food on magnetic trays. The magnetic tray means that the knives, forks and spoons stick to the trays and don't float away. A straw is used for drinks.

Astronauts sleep in sleeping bags attached to the walls of the station. They zip themselves in so they don't float out of the bag while asleep.

1 d **2** c **3** b **4** a

Pg 41

Although people have already walked on the Moon, there are plans for further exploration, and even a permanent settlement, on the Moon.

Some people believe that the Moon is a ready-made space station. Further exploration of space could occur from a Moon base. As there is less gravity, spacecraft would need less energy to take off from the Moon than they do from Earth.

Water ice has been discovered at the Moon's poles. This could be melted for drinking water, and broken down into oxygen for breathing and hydrogen for nuclear fuel.

The south pole of the Moon is an ideal position for a base. This site can provide water ice. There is also a mountain which receives almost continuous sunlight. If solar panels were installed, a Moon base could use solar energy.

5 Both Earth and the Moon receive sunlight, have gravity and ice.
6 There are no permanent settlements on the Moon. There is less gravity on the Moon than on Earth. There is ice on the Moon but no running water. People don't currently live on the Moon.

Lesson 197

Pg 42

Healthy, productive land can become dry and salty because of the way people use two natural resources: soil and water.

Trees and other plants bind soil together with their root systems. When too much native vegetation is removed — such as when land is cleared to graze animals — the structure of the soil breaks down. It dries out and erodes, either blown away by the wind or carried away by rain.

Soil can become compacted by overgrazing from cattle and other domesticated animals.

1 b **2** a **3** a **4** d **5** a

Pg 43

Industries make products and materials, such as electricity and fuel, which provide us with a modern, comfortable way of life — but they also pollute our natural resources.

The major sources of industrial air pollution are chemical plants, power stations, oil refineries and factories. However, cars pollute the air as much as industries do.

Under certain weather conditions, several air pollutants can have a combined effect that is worse than their individual effects. An example is photochemical smog, sometimes seen as a white haze over cities during summer. Photochemical smog forms on still days when sunlight drives chemical reactors between fuels and chemicals into the air. A product of these reactions is ozone, a gas harmful to people, animals and plants.

6 Positive—makes life more comfortable for us. Negative—pollutes natural resources.
7 chemical plants, power stations, oil refineries, factories, cars
8 On still days, sunlight drives chemical reactors between fuels and chemicals into the air causing the formation of the ozone.

Lesson 198

Pg 44

Even when it's not the planting or harvesting seasons, crops still need constant attention, like watering, fertilising and pruning. Some crops require more care than others. The time needed for each crop will also depend on the weather, time of year and how long the crop has been growing.

Crops need fertilising to encourage growth. Pruning controls unwanted growth so trees can bear the most fruit possible. Watering and fertilising also help crops grow to their best potential.

Farmers use fertilisers as a way of adding nutrients already present in the soil. Fertilisers can be a huge expense for farmers, so it is very important to apply it in the right amounts at the right time to maintain a profitable farm.

1 d **2** c, d, f

Pg 45

A banana plant produces fruit about 15–18 months after planting. A banana bunch is ready for picking when the fruit is still green but just starting to yellow.

Harvesting bananas is hard work — bunches of bananas often weigh more than 50 kg. During the harvest season, two cutters and a driver go around the plantation cutting down the fruit and stacking them on a trailer. When transporting bananas, we always use padding to protect the skins from bruising.

Back at the shed, we hang up the bunches of bananas. Technology today makes this process a whole lot easier. We use a hydraulic lift, whereas a few years ago we had to carry the bunches on our backs!

3 harvesting bananas
4 Teacher check

Lesson 199

Pg 46

1 a, b **2** d **3** b

Pg 47

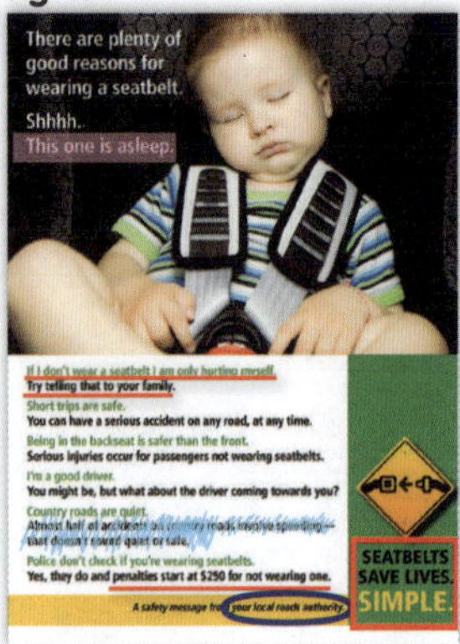

4 the general public **5** Teacher check

6 The picture appeals to our emotions. The child is innocent and vulnerable. Drivers would not want to put the child's life at risk.

Lesson 200

Pg 48

1 c **2** b **3** a **4** d

Pg 49

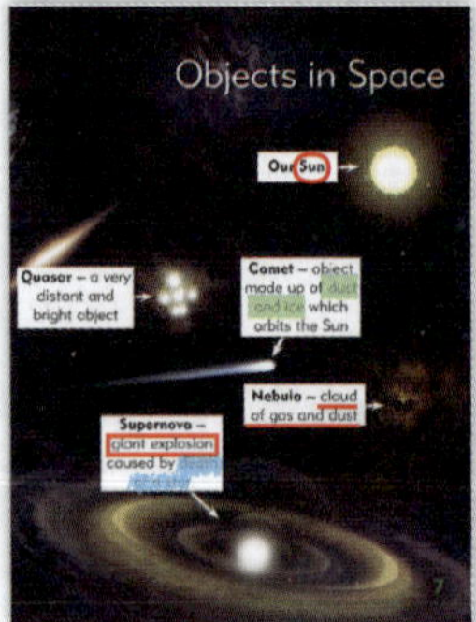

5 Teacher check **6** Teacher check

7 Teacher check

Grammar Lesson 4

Pg 50

Africa

Africa is the second largest continent on Earth. It contains more than 50 countries.

North Africa is mostly dry and features Mount Kilimanjaro and the Sahara, the world's largest hot desert.

Central Africa is crossed by the equator. The warm rain forests of this region are home to many rare animals such as forest elephants and leopards.

Southern Africa has many mines. They provide a major portion of the world's 12 main mineral resources.

Africa has the second highest population in the world, including hundreds of different ethnic groups. More than 2000 languages are spoken here.

1 c **2** a **3** c **4** b **5** d

Pg 51

6 b, c, f

7 a is spoken **b** is worn **c** is grown **d** have been created **e** was elected

8 a We were made to feel welcome by the Zambian people.

b The tourists were given directions by the African people.

c The African village is being rebuilt by a group of volunteers.

Assessment 2

Pg 52–53

1 c **2** b **3** d **4** b **5** c **6** a **7** b **8** d

9 Teacher check **10** Teacher check

Lesson 201

Pg 54

Life goes on as usual, except that I have started working at Chicken Heaven. I am nervous about learning the codes for different meals on the cash register but I enjoy it. I am so motivated I even do my homework and make my bed without being nagged.

Finally it is Tuesday. My grandmother is due home today. I am stuck at school and the day drags. I have trouble concentrating. The second my last class finishes, I am out the door. I ride home at a speed that an Olympic cyclist would envy.

1 a, c, d **2** b, d

Pg 55

I nod, unable to imagine my brother Troy with the Eye. A week ago I wouldn't have imagined myself with the Eye either. "Do you still have normal dreams too? I mean weird dreams that can't possibly come true?"

My grandmother smiles. "Yes, I still have those. They keep me on my toes."

I sip my hot chocolate. "Is there anything I can do about the Eye?"

My grandmother laughs. "You can't turn it off, if that's what you mean." She becomes serious. "You must learn to live with it. Don't try to fight it."

3 Teacher check **4** Teacher check

Lesson 202

Pg 56

The busy harbour was strangely deserted! None of the fishing boats were in port and the cafes were empty. The only person they could see was an old Greek lady outside one of the cafes. She was hanging squid on lines to dry in the sun.

"Hello," said Mia as they approached her. "My name's Mia and this is Flynn. Where is everyone?"

"They're all at the celebrations," she said, turning and offering them a seat. "I can't stand the crowds myself."

The old lady pointed out to sea. "Today is the day the fishermen take all the villagers out to sea. They give thanks to the god of the sea, Poseidon, for good fishing."

1 d **2** b

Pg 57

The old lady's eyes lit up as she leaned closer. "Legend has it that the mighty sea god, Poseidon, made Atlantis for a woman he loved. Atlantis was a rich and beautiful place with silver topped temples, grand palaces, winding canals, magnificent harbours and lots of exotic animals."

"So what happened?" urged Flynn.

"Well, it seems the Atlanteans, who had everything they could wish for, became greedy and corrupt. Zeus, the king of all the gods, was so angry with them he banished the island to the bottom of the sea."

3 Teacher check

Lesson 203

Remarks by the President of the United States of America on Pardoning of the National Turkey

******

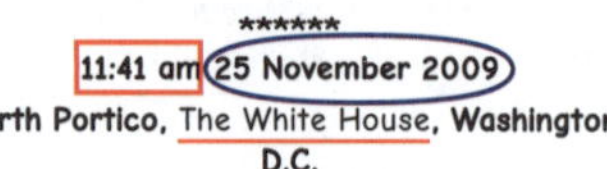
11:41 am 25 November 2009

North Portico, The White House, Washington D.C.

******

Happy Thanksgiving, everybody. Welcome to the White House. On behalf of Sasha and Malia and myself, we're thrilled to see you. I want to thank Walter Pelletier, chairman of the National Turkey Federation, and Joel Brandenberger, its president, for donating this year's turkey.

Pg 58

1 c **2** a **3** b **4** d

Pg 59

You know, there are certain days that remind me of why I ran for this office. And then there are moments like this — (laughter) — where I pardon a turkey and send it to Disneyland. (Laughter) But every single day, I am thankful for the extraordinary responsibility that the American people have placed in me. I am humbled by the privilege that it is to serve them and the tremendous honour it is to serve as Commander-in Chief of the finest military in the world — and I want to wish a Happy Thanksgiving to every service member at home or in harm's way. We're proud of you and we are thinking of you and we're praying for you.

5 to Disneyland

6 the responsibility placed in him by the American people

7 the privilege of being able to serve the American people

8 Commander-in-Chief

Lesson 204

Pg 60

Mum: Jack, Nanna needs help down the stairs.

Jack: That's my job. Three flights.

LFX Stairs.

Jack: Come on, Nan, give us your arm. She had a bad fall last year and broke her arm. Oh, don't worry, she can't hear, she's deaf.

He becomes Nanna struggling to go down the stairs.

Nanna: Have you got me, Jack? Oh, it's been a lovely afternoon. Do you like my new teeth? I've just had them renovated. I've eaten too many cookies. Hope they don't repeat. I won't be needing m'tea. Oh dear ... these stairs. I swear if I trip, I'll roll all the way down to the bottom.

Nanna wobbles. He transforms back to Jack.

Jack: Are you alright, Nan?

1 b **2** d **3** a, d

Pg 61

Jack encounters Mum doing star jumps in the kitchen.

Mum hates her thighs and the tops of her arms, so she's always doing star jumps, even in the middle of making dinner. Her hair fluffs up when she jumps. It's pretty funny. It wasn't so funny when Mum did it in the school car park the other day. What if someone saw her?

Mum: What, darling?

Jack: Don't call me that.

Mum: But you are my darling.

Jack: Mum, you promised, never again. I need to talk to you. Now.

Mum: When I've finished making dinner.

SFX Volcano begins.

That's a joke. Rob'll be here soon and then there'll be dinner, washing up, shower, homework. There'll be no time and I HAVE to talk to her. I think I'm in BIG trouble.

4 She hopes doing star jumps will improve the look of her thighs and the tops of her arms.
5 jumping up and down
6 Mum calls him "darling"

Lesson 205

Pg 62

Long ago, there was a Seneca boy who had been hunting in the forest all day. He sat on a stone to rest. As he sat, he heard a voice say, "Shall I tell you a story?"

The boy looked around to see who was talking to him. He could see no one. The voice spoke again. "Shall I tell you a story?" This time the boy realized that the voice was coming from the stone he was sitting on.

The boy wondered about the things the stone could tell. "Yes, I would like you to tell me a story," said the boy.

"First, you must give me one of the birds you caught today," said the stone.

The boy laid down one of his birds and the stone began. It told stories about strange creatures called stone giants, and flying heads that used to make war on the Seneca people.

1 Teacher check

Pg 63

As soon as the stone finished one story, it began another. The boy was spellbound.

Day after day for weeks, the boy returned, always swapping a bird for the stone's stories. He began to bring people from his village with him. Soon lots of people were coming to the stone to hear its stories. Then, one day the stone said to the boy, "I will no longer tell stories. Now it is your job to remember them and tell them to your people. Wherever you go to tell these legends, you will be welcomed and cared for."

The boy was given gifts in every Seneca village, just as he had given the stone a gift each day. He spread the stories among his people until he died. The stories are still told today.

2 Teacher check

Grammar Lesson 5

Pg 64

The Sit-in

I felt a tug on my sleeve and turned around. It was Billy, who just smiled. I tried to smile back, but I was worried that we were all about to lose our jobs.

The workers chose three men who would speak on their behalf. For hours they negotiated with Mr Perkins, while the rest of us remained sitting.

Finally, one of the workers returned and announced that four windows upstairs would stay open all day, and that the girls on my line could have two twenty-minute breaks during our twelve-hour shift.

With a show of hands, we voted to go back to work. No one saw much of Mr Perkins for the rest of the day. There was a rumour that he went home because he had lost his voice.

1 b 2 b 3 b 4 a 5 c

Pg 65

6 a Molly wanted to complain to Mr Perkins, but she was afraid of losing her job.
b Molly had to work in the soap factory, or her family would starve.
c Molly walked past Mr Perkins and joined the sit-in.
d Mr Perkins yelled at Molly and made her stay back for no pay.
e Mr Perkins was angry, but he listened to their complaints.

7 a Mr Perkins was angry because Molly was late.
b Molly worked in a factory that produced soap.
c Molly was upset when Mr Perkins yelled at her.
d Molly saw a woman who was handing out pamphlets.
e Mr Perkins threatened to sack everyone if they didn't get back to work.

8 Teacher check

Lesson 206

Pg 66

Space stations allow people to live in space for long periods of time. Supporters believe that space exploration benefits people on Earth. Other people are worried about the cost of a space station and whether the discoveries are worthwhile.

The International Space Station (ISS) is the biggest structure ever built in space. Due to its size, people can live and work on the ISS for much longer than ever before. This allows scientists to gather information about the effects of living in space for long periods. This information could be helpful in working through the challenges of travelling to Mars.

1 c 2 b 3 a 4 d

Pg 67

Distances in space are measured in light years. This is the distance that light travels in one year.

A ray of light travels about 9.5 trillion kilometres in one year, or 9.5 million million kilometres—9 500 000 000 000 km. Scientists use light years to measure distances in the universe. They use light years to measure distances between galaxies and between stars.

Light years also tell how long the light has taken to reach Earth. Alpha Centauri is one of the closest stars to Earth. It is 4.3 light years from Earth. This means that the light from this star has taken 4.3 years to reach Earth. We see the star as it was 4.3 years ago.

5 Light travels very quickly—"A ray of light travels about 9.5 trillion kilometres in one year."
6 Distances in space are enormous—it takes the light from one of our closest stars "4.3 years to reach Earth."

Lesson 207

Pg 68

Darkness and the iron testing rod told us that there was empty space. Perhaps another descending staircase, in accordance to the ordinary royal Theban tomb plan? Or maybe a chamber? Candles were procured—the all important tell-tale for foul gases when opening an ancient subterranean excavation — I widened the breach and by means of the candle looked in, while Lord Carnarvon, Lady E., and Callender with the Reises waited in anxious expectation.

1 a descending b procured
c subterranean d excavation

2 a descending—going down
b procured—obtained
c subterranean—beneath the earthy underground
d excavation—a site that has been hollowed out

Pg 69

Our sensations and astonishment are difficult to describe, as the better light revealed to us the marvellous collection of treasures: two strange ebony-black effigies of a King, gold sandalled, bearing staff and mace, loomed out from the cloak of darkness; gilded couches in strange forms, lion-headed, Hathor-headed and beast infernal; exquisitely painted, inlaid and ornamental caskets; flowers; strange black shrines with a gilded monster snake appearing from within; quite ordinary-looking, white chests; finely carved chairs; a golden, inlaid throne; a heap of large, curious, white oviform boxes; beneath our very eyes, on the threshold, a lovely lotiform wishing-cup in translucent alabaster.

3 a sensations b effigies
c oviform d translucent

4 a sensations—feelings
b effigies—models, sculptures
c oviform—egg-shaped
d translucent—see-through

Lesson 208

Pg 70

A call comes in on my pager—MAJOR TRAUMA—HELIPAD. ARRIVAL 2 MINUTES.

Along with an Emergency Room (ER) doctor, I rush to the helipad. The helicopter doors open and the patient, a 19-year-old male lying on a stretcher, is rushed into the hospital.

On the way down to the ER, the paramedic begins his report, "... high-speed car accident ... unconscious at the scene ... tachycardic ... extensive blood loss ..."

Once inside the ER, we transfer the patient to a resuscitation bay (resus bay) and we are joined by the rest of the trauma team and an anesthesiologist. We try to stabilise the patient as our team's assessment begins.

1 6, 2, 9, 1, 5, 7, 3, 4, 8

Pg 71

The patient cannot breathe properly, so we decide to put a breathing tube down his throat and into his lungs to allow a ventilator to breathe for him.

The doctor signals that it is time to administer the medications to sedate and paralyse the patient. This is so he feels no pain. The doctor puts the tube down the patient's throat and his chest starts to rise and fall more easily with the help of the ventilator. A chest X-ray is taken to make sure the tube is in the right place and inflating both lungs correctly.

The patient is now stable enough to transfer to radiology for further scans to check for possible neck and head injuries.

2 The patient is having difficulty breathing and is placed on a ventilator. Inserting the tube down the patient's throat and into his lungs can be a painful experience, so first he must be sedated. With the tube in, the patient is able to breathe more easily. Once he has been stabilised, he is moved to radiology. The patient needs further scans to check for possible injuries.

ANSWERS • PAGES 72–83

Lesson 209

Pg 72

Dear Resident,

The survey below is part of a project to help understand and build the local community. It is being given to each household in the Trevally district.

About living in Trevally

1 How long have you been at your current address in the Trevally district? (Please check a box.)

- [ ] Less than 12 months
- [x] 1–2 years
- [ ] 5–10 years
- [ ] more than 10 years

2 How much do you agree with the following statements? (Please circle a number.)
1 = strongly disagree 7 = strongly agree

a) When I go shopping I am likely to meet friends and acquaintances.
1 2 (3) 4 5 6 7

b) It is safe to walk around the area at night.
1 2 3 4 5 6 (7)

1 a F b F **2** a F b F c O

Pg 73

Please complete the survey and put it in the mail by Friday, 31 August in the reply paid envelope provided.

Your life experience

4 How much do you agree with the following statements? (Please circle a number.)
1 = disagree strongly 7 = agree strongly

a) I am happy about my housing situation.
1 2 3 4 5 6 (7)

b) In general, I have excellent health.
1 2 3 4 (5) 6 7

c) I often feel rushed, pressured and too busy.
(1) 2 3 4 5 6 7

3 "in the mail by Friday, 31 August" and "in the reply paid envelope provided"

4 The resident is very happy with his or her situation.

5 The resident believes that his or her health is very good.

6 The resident does not think he or she ever feels rushed, pressured or too busy.

Lesson 210

Pg 74

Farmers use chemical fertilisers and pesticides on their crops. When it rains, some of these chemicals may wash into rivers. This can cause algal bloom in lakes and rivers. Algal bloom is the rapid growth of algae on the water's surface. It blocks out sunlight and uses up oxygen in the water. Fish and plants need oxygen to live, so algal bloom can kill them. Some algae are poisonous and make the water undrinkable.

When heavily polluted air mixes with the water in clouds, it falls back to earth as acid rain. Acid rain can make the soil so acidic that trees can't grow.

1 b **2** d **3** a **4** b **5** b

Pg 75

Wetlands act as natural water filters. They are like sponges, with the soil holding large amounts of water. When there is heavy rain, wetlands absorb the water and then release it slowly later. This helps prevent flooding of surrounding land.

Wetlands were once seen as damp, dangerous places that caused diseases. They were used as dumping grounds for trash and sewage, and many wetlands were destroyed to create more land for agriculture and building.

Heavy rain then went straight into rivers, rather than wetlands, and contributed to flooding. Because wetlands are breeding grounds for fish and other aquatic life, the loss of wetlands damaged fishing industries.

6 They thought the wetlands were damp, dangerous places that caused diseases.

7 They were destroyed to create more land for agriculture and building.

8 Wetlands are breeding grounds for fish, so their destruction damaged fishing industries. Flooding occurred because instead of going into wetlands, heavy rain went straight into rivers.

Grammar Lesson 6

Pg 76

Emma Watson

Emma Charlotte Duerre Watson was born in Paris and brought up in Oxfordshire. She landed the role of Hermione Granger in the *Harry Potter* films when she was just nine years old. She spent the next ten years, during which she completed primary and high school, acting in eight *Harry Potter* films.

Watson uses her position as a United Nations Goodwill Ambassador to promote the UN's HeForShe campaign, which asks men and boys to speak out against gender inequality.

Supporters make the following statement and commitment when they sign up: "I am one of billions of men who believe equality for women is a basic human right that benefits us all. And I commit to taking action against gender discrimination and violence in order to build a more just and equal world."

1 d **2** c **3** c **4** a **5** b

Pg 77

6 a J K Rowling is the author who wrote the Harry Potter books.
b Hermione attended Hogwarts, where she met Harry and Ron.
c Watson has been nominated for awards, many of which she has won.
d I told him about the movie that Emma Watson acts in.
e I have read the Harry Potter books, which are all bestsellers.

7 a whose photo is on the poster
b which are extremely popular
c who is a bestselling author

8 a Emma Watson visited Zambia where she promoted education for girls.
b The man who is concerned about gender equality has joined HeForShe.
c I belong to the organisation that promotes gender equality.
d The man whose beliefs I share is a volunteer for HeForShe.

Assessment 3

Pg 78–79

1 c **2** a **3** b **4** d **5** b **6** d **7** c **8** b
9 Teacher check **10** Teacher check

Lesson 211

Pg 80

"Oh, I can't work with you," said Hannah. "This is insane. I need some air." She grabbed her books and looked out the window. "I'm going to sit under that tree."

"Wh...? Wha...? What tree?" stammered Josh. Hannah was already out the door and headed for his snake tree. All he could do was watch through the window as she walked down the stairs and sat right under the branch. He couldn't help but notice how undead the snake looked. Normally, he would have been pleased. Right now, he felt sick. Josh reckoned it would take Hannah about three seconds to notice the snake. He began to count. "AAAAAAAAAAHHHHHHHHHHHHHHHHHHHHHHH!"

1 b **2** c **3** d **4** b **5** a

Pg 81

Hannah sat with Emma, a girl from the year above. Josh hid in the seat behind Hannah, waiting for another chance to talk to her. Then he overheard Hannah's plan.

"That is such a good idea," cried Hannah with excitement. "It gets me out of working with Super Pain and I'm not cheating or breaking any of the Assignment Quest rules."

"Exactly," agreed Emma. "You're still working in a team and you're not swapping him for someone else. You're just getting him to do what he's best at—which in this case isn't much."

They both giggled.

Josh heard Hannah say, "So what's the web address for this site, Emma? I'd better write it down."

6 He was waiting for another chance to talk to her.

7 Emma had told Hannah how she could get out of working with Josh without cheating or breaking any of the Assignment Quest Rules.

8 Emma's comment about getting Josh to do what he was best at—in this case, not much

Lesson 212

Pg 82

School was even more complicated than home. Rory enjoyed school. He knew the answers to most of the questions Mr Logie asked the class, but everyone was always in such a hurry.

"Today we are going to learn about coal," began Mr Logie warily, trying not to look in Rory's direction. But Rory's arm shot up and waved about. Mr Logie decided to risk it. "Yes, what is it, Rory?"

"Please, sir, will we be learning about black coal, brown coal or charcoal?"

"Coal!" thundered Mr Logie. JUST—ABOUT—COAL! And I am warning you, Rory! I happen to think that sending complicated-boys-who-ask-too-many-questions down coal mines is A VERY GOOD IDEA!"

1 b **2** d **3** a **4** c

Pg 83

By this time, Lettice was ready to play with her ridiculous dog called Parrot.

Sorry to be rude about a small animal, but she was ridiculous. She looked like a parrot without feathers. She even had a crest like a parrot. Rory gawped the first time he saw Parrot and wondered what unpleasant disease she had.

"Chinese Crested!" said Lettice. "Very simple—no brushing, no fleas, no walking. And she makes a good hot water bottle."

"It looks very ... er, um, fragile," said Rory, trying to be polite.

Lettice giggled. "Hideous, you mean! But I love her."

5 The author thinks Parrot the dog is ridiculous—"She looked like a parrot without feathers".

6 Rory thought there was something strange about Lettice's dog. The first time he saw her he "wondered what unpleasant disease she had".

7 Lettice agrees that her dog looks "hideous", but says she loves her nevertheless. She says Parrot is easy to take care of, and makes a good hot water bottle.

Lesson 213

Pg 84

Text 1

As they neared the Abbey, Robin walked in front of the rest and held his bow in his free hand. Presently he came to a stream and heard sounds of a jovial song floating towards him. He hid under a bush and watched alertly. At length, approaching the far bank, Robin espied a knight, clad in chain armour and very merry. He sang, in a lusty voice, a hearty woodland song. "Now by my bones!" thought Robin, puzzled, "but I have heard this song before."

Text 2

Steadily Robin pressed forward till he came to a stream that dipped in and out among the willows and rushes on the banks.

As he sat down to rest and take his bearings, he heard snatches of a jovial song floating to him from the farther side.

Presently the willows on the other bank parted and there emerged a stout friar in a long cloak, tied with a cord in the middle. On his head was a knight's helmet and in his hand was a huge pasty pie.

1 c **2** b **3** d **4** a

Pg 85

Text 1

Robin called out suddenly upon the knight, fitting an arrow as he did so.

"I pray you, Sir Knight, to carry me across this stream," said Robin.

"Put down your bow, forester," shouted the knight, "and I will safely carry you across the stream."

While Robin was searching his memory to fit a name to this courteous knight, the latter had waded across to him.

The knight carried Robin safely across the stream.

"Now, gossip, you shall carry me over this stream," said the knight serenely. "One good turn deserves another, as you know."

Text 2

Robin seized his bow and fitted an arrow. "Hey, Friar!" he sang out, "carry me over the water."

"Put down your bow, fellow," the friar shouted back, "and I will bring you over the stream."

The friar waded across the stream and took Robin upon his back. He spoke neither good word nor bad till he came to the other side.

Robin leaped lightly off his back, and said, "I am much beholden to you good father."

"Beholden, say you!" rejoined the other, drawing his sword; "then you shall repay your score. In short, my son, you must carry me back again."

5. Robin fits an arrow to his bow and asks the man to carry him across the stream. The man agrees to Robin's request, but says Robin must first put down his bow. When they get to the other side, the man says Robin must carry him back.
6. Text 1: the man is a knight; Robin hides under a bush; Robin thinks he recognises the man
   Text 2: the man is a friar

Lesson 214

Pg 86

I will arise and go now, and go to Innisfree,
And a small cabin build there, of clay and wattles made:
Nine bean-rows will I have there, a hive for the honey-bee;
And live alone on the bee-loud glade.

And I shall have some peace there, for peace comes dropping slow,
Dropping from the veils of the morning to where the cricket sings;
There midnight's all a glimmer, and noon a purple glow,
And evening full of the linnet's wings.

1 b **2** c **3** a **4** a, b

Pg 87

And I shall have some peace there, for peace comes dropping slow,
Dropping from the veils of the morning to where the cricket sings;
There midnight's all a glimmer, and noon a purple glow,
And evening full of the linnet's wings.

I will arise and go now, for always night and day
I hear lake water lapping with low sounds by the shore;
While I stand on the roadway, or on the pavements grey,
I hear it in the deep heart's core.

5. Teacher check
6. alliteration
7. They are soft sounds, like the sound of water gently lapping on the shore.

Lesson 215

Pg 88

King Minos was filled with anger. The hero, Theseus, had killed the Minotaur in a labyrinth and had now escaped. The King blamed the master craftsman, Daedalus, for helping Theseus. He ordered that Daedalus be trapped in a tower of the labyrinth he had designed and built, on the island of Crete.

"As extra punishment, your son can join you!" roared King Minos.

1 b **2** c **3** a **4** d

Pg 89

After a year, Daedalus had made two pairs of wings. He strapped one set of wings on himself and the other onto his son.

"Stay close to me, Icarus," said Daedalus. "Listen carefully — do not fly so low that the sea spray soaks the feathers or so high that the sun melts the wax." He showed his son how to flap his arms so the wings beat the air, and together they rose to freedom and away from the tower.

Icarus was excited as the earth fell away, filled with the thrill of flying and finally being free. He began to be careless. Unable to contain his excitement, he flew higher and higher. Icarus completely forgot his father's warning.

5. Daedalus was a talented craftsman—he "made two pairs of wings" that allowed him and his son to fly.
6. The wings could be destroyed. Daedalus warned Icarus that "sea spray soaks the feathers" and "the sun melts the wax".
7. Icarus' wings would most likely be destroyed by the sun—"he flew higher and higher".

Grammar Lesson 7

Pg 90

A Safer Place to Hide

The eye of the storm is passing over us," said Uncle Lou. "We don't have a lot of time. We must go downstairs to the laundry."

"Uncle Lou's right," said Dad. "We can't stay here. If the rest of the house goes, the laundry's our best chance."

With his torch, Dad led the way out of the bathroom. The inside of the house was a mess. The Christmas tree had blown across the room, and now the tip of it was wedged under the fridge. Broken furniture and glass lay everywhere. All the windows were broken. Everything was wet.

Uncle Lou was already outside. "Be careful of the stairs, they aren't holding on by much."

Mum carried Baxter and cautiously made her way down.

1 b **2** c **3** d **4** b **5** a

Pg 91

6. Teacher check
7. **a** given **b** studying **c** do **d** can **e** should **f** don't **g** been
8. **a** had ripped **b** were blowing **c** had washed **d** had been destroyed **e** had been left **f** were overflowing **g** would be evacuated

Lesson 216

Pg 92

As I read through the articles for the summer issue, I notice there's an interesting one on making skateboards and another on secret beach huts that kids have built. Both are great for the summer issue.

There's a huge buzz around the summer issue — and this one is shaping up to be our biggest ever. Our readers and advertisers look forward to it as we always try to do something to make these issues different and collectable. We have a few surprises in the pipeline — which is a good sign.

Putting together this issue can take eight months to plan and organise. This is fairly stressful as we still have to publish the monthly issues of *Hive* in the meantime.

1 c **2** d **3** b **4** a

Pg 93

Early magazines did not restrict themselves to leisure interests but often had political and religious content. In the mid-1700s, magazines did not always have what we now see as covers. Many had their cover page as a table of contents, or they began an article on the cover. The first teen magazines appeared in America and England in the 1940s.

There's now a magazine for practically every imaginable interest, from fashion or food, to football or fishing.

There are more magazines today than ever before. Magazines both inform and entertain. It's this magical combination that has kept sales rising for nearly 300 years.

5. Early magazines—cover page a table of contents, or start of an article; often mixed leisure interests with political and religious content
   Modern magazines—cater for many different interests; special covers
6. Modern magazines aim to inform and entertain and so did early magazines.

ANSWERS • PAGES 94–105

Lesson 217

Pg 94

Plastic stamped with identification code 1 are PET (polyethylene terephthalate) plastics, often used as soft drink, water and juice bottles.

PET bottles are recycled by separating them from other types of plastic, and sorting them into different colour groups: clear, blue and green, and a mixed colour group.

They are then crushed and transported to the recycler.

Once there, they are sorted again, washed and then shredded into flakes. The flakes are washed, dried and melted to make new plastic products: fleece clothing, pillows, carpets, ropes, sleeping bags, life jackets, furniture, building materials — and more PET bottles.

1 b **2** d **3** a **4** b **5** a

Pg 95

Glass for recycling is sorted by colour: clear, amber and green. Materials that contaminate the glass, such as metal bottle tops, are removed.

The glass is crushed into cullet. Cullet is often mixed with the raw materials of glass (sand, soda ash and limestone) before being melted in a furnace at up to 1500° Celsius.

The molten glass is poured into moulding machines and air is blown through it to shape new glass products. These are cooled down slowly before they can be used.

6 **a** sort the glass by colour.
b materials that contaminate the glass are removed.
c the glass is crushed into cullet.
d placing it in a furnace at up to 1500°Celcius.
e the molten glass is poured into moulding machines and air is blown through it to shape the new glass products.
f is to let the new glass products cool down.

Lesson 218

Pg 96

Almost all of our electricity comes from burning fossil fuels: coal, natural gas and oil. Power companies can make burning coal a cleaner process by washing coal before burning it. They can also burn a type of coal that contains less pollution-producing sulphur, or use devices called "scrubbers" to remove sulphur dioxide from the gas that leaves the power plant.

Individuals can also have a major effect on reducing pollution. People can use less electricity and choose "green power" — electricity that comes from non-polluting sources, such as hydro-electricity and wind farms.

1 c **2** a **3** b **4** c **5** d

Pg 97

Scientists predict that global warming will cause massive changes to the environment. These changes will affect everyone — where they live, how they travel and the cost of living.

It is difficult to predict the exact effects of global warming. How quickly the climate will change depends on how much greenhouse gas emissions grow, and how sensitive the climate is to these emissions.

Extremes of weather have been predicted — more frequent and intense heatwaves, storms, floods and droughts. Farms would yield fewer crops. Rising ocean levels, from melting ice caps, could force millions of people from their homes.

6 Global warming will cause huge changes to the environment. We could have more frequent and intense heatwaves, storms, floods and droughts. This will affect everyone's lives. Farms will produce fewer crops and melting ice caps will cause oceans to rise, forcing millions of people from their homes.

Lesson 219

Pg 98

Journal entry of Joseph Banks — 11 June 1770

... the tide ebbed so much that we found it impossible to attempt to get [the ship] off till next high water, if she would hold together so long; and we now found to add to our misfortune that we had got ashore nearly at the top of high water and as night tides generally rise higher than day ones we had little hopes of getting off even then.

Journal entry of Captain James Cook — 11 June 1770

Before 10 o'clock we had 20 and 21 fathoms, and continued in that depth until a few minutes before 11, when we had 17, and before the man at the lead could heave another cast, the ship struck and stuck fast. Immediately upon this we took in all our sails, hoisted out the boats and sounded round the ship, and found that we had got upon the south-east edge of a reef of coral rocks.

1 b **2** d **3** a **4** a

Pg 99

Joseph Banks's journal entry

Orders were now given for lightening the ship, which began by starting our water and pumping it up; the ballast was then got up and thrown over board, as well as 6 of our guns (all that we had upon deck).

At night the tide almost floated her but she made water so fast that three pumps hard worked could but just keep her clear. Now, in my own opinion I entirely gave up the ship and, packing up what I thought I might save, prepared myself for the worst.

Captain Cook's journal entry

As we went ashore about the top of high water we not only started water, but threw overboard our guns, iron and stone ballast, casks, hoop staves, oil jars, decayed stores, etc.; many of these last articles lay in the way at coming at heavier. All this time the ship made little or no water. At 11 am, being high water as we thought, we tried to heave her off without success, she not being afloat by a foot or more, notwithstanding by this time we had thrown overboard 40 or 50 tonnes of weight.

5 The sailors made the ship lighter by throwing overboard guns, iron and stone ballasts, casks, hoop staves, oil jars, decayed stores, etc.

6 Joseph Banks's account is more personal. He tells how he felt about their situation — that he had given up hope and was preparing for the worst.

Lesson 220

Pg 100

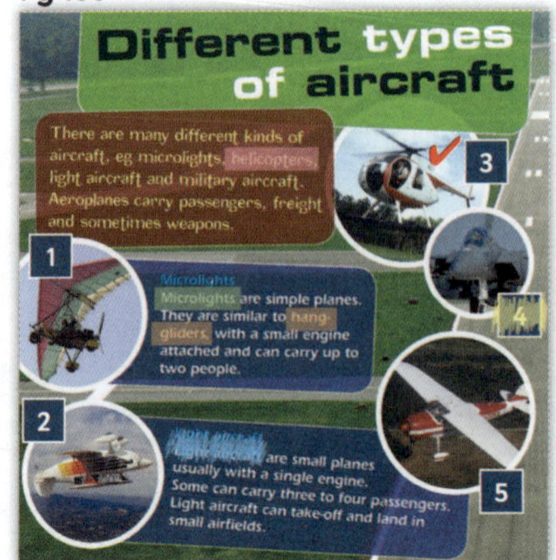

1 c **2** c **3** d **4** a

Pg 101

Aircraft instruments

Aircraft have instruments to provide the pilot with important information.

Basic aircraft instruments include:

- airspeed indicator — indicates how fast the plane is moving through the air
- altimeter — indicates the altitude of the aircraft, above the ground or above sea level
- attitude indicator — also called an artificial horizon, indicates the exact orientation of the plane as it pitches and rolls through the air.

Modern aeroplanes have lots of instruments to keep track of!

Keeping yourself the right way up — even when you can't see anything!

5 They give the reader a better understanding of the text by showing him or her what the instruments look like.

6 Some of the instruments have pictures of planes on them.

7 A large passenger plane has two pilots.

Grammar Lesson 8

Pg 102

Robots to the Rescue

Nanorobots, or nanobots, are very, very small robots — smaller than the width of a human hair.

Nanobots are still in the development stage. They are expected to revolutionise the way doctors treat diseases.

In the future, scientists believe that doctors will inject nanobots into our blood. The nanobots will swim through our bodies, looking for signs of illness. If, for instance, they detect a virus, they will destroy it before it makes us sick. In addition, these little helpers will give us medicine when we need it.

Some scientists are even predicting that in the future, people won't grow old. As soon as our cells show signs of wear and tear, nanobots will replace them with healthy ones.

1 b **2** d **3** c **4** b **5** c

Pg 103

6 **a** will **b** is **c** be **d** am **e** will

7 **a** will be **b** are going to listen
c will change **d** will be done
e will be fitted **f** will take over
g will have built

8 Teacher check

Assessment 4

Pg 104–105

1 d **2** c **3** a, c **4** c **5** c **6** b **7** c **8** b
9 Teacher check **10** Teacher check